LYRICS OF LOYALTY.

The Red, White, and Blue Series.

IN PRESS:

Uniform with this Volume.

I.

SONGS OF THE SOLDIERS.

II.

PERSONAL AND POLITICAL BALLADS OF THE WAR.

LYRICS OF LOYALTY

ARRANGED AND EDITED BY

FRANK MOORE

NEW YORK
GEORGE P. PUTNAM
1864

RIVERSIDE, CAMBRIDGE:
STEREOTYPED AND PRINTED BY H. O. HOUGHTON.

NOTE.

The purpose of this collection is to preserve some of the best specimens of the Lyrical Writings which the present Rebellion has called forth. The limited space afforded by a single volume has compelled the editor to enlarge the work by adding a Second and a Third Series, which will be issued at an early day. The Second Series will embrace the Songs of the Soldiers, and Ballads of the Rebellion; while the Personal and Political epics and rhymes, which have been produced on the Rebel as well as National side of the contest, will be given in the Third Series.

F. M.

New York, December, 1863.

CONTENTS.

LIST OF AUTHORS.

LYRICS OF LOYALTY.

OUR COUNTRY'S CALL.

BY WILLIAM CULLEN BRYANT.

LAY down the axe, fling by the spade :
Leave in its track the toiling plough;
The rifle and the bayonet-blade
For arms like yours were fitter now;
And let the hands that ply the pen
Quit the light task, and learn to wield
The horseman's crooked brand, and rein
The charger on the battle-field.

Our country calls; away! away!
To where the blood-stream blots the green.
Strike to defend the gentlest sway
That Time in all his course has seen.

See, from a thousand coverts — see
  Spring the armed foes that haunt her track;
They rush to smite her down, and we
  Must beat the banded traitors back.

Ho! sturdy as the oaks ye cleave,
  And moved as soon to fear and flight,
Men of the glade and forest! leave
  Your woodcraft for the field of fight.
The arms that wield the axe must pour
  An iron tempest on the foe;
His serried ranks shall reel before
  The arm that lays the panther low.

And ye who breast the mountain storm
  By grassy steep or highland lake,
Come, for the land ye love, to form
  A bulwark that no foe can break.
Stand, like your own gray cliffs that mock
  The whirlwind; stand in her defence:
The blast as soon shall move the rock
  As rushing squadrons bear ye thence.

And ye, whose homes are by her grand
  Swift rivers, rising far away,
Come from the depth of her green land
  As mighty in your march as they;

As terrible as when the rains
  Have swelled them over bank and bourne,
With sudden floods to drown the plains
  And sweep along the woods uptorn.

And ye who throng, beside the deep,
  Her ports and hamlets of the strand,
In number like the waves that leap
  On his long murmuring marge of sand,
Come, like that deep, when, o'er his brim,
  He rises, all his floods to pour,
And flings the proudest barks that swim,
  A helpless wreck against his shore.

Few, few were they whose swords, of old,
  Won the fair land in which we dwell;
But we are many, we who hold
  The grim resolve to guard it well.
Strike for that broad and goodly land,
  Blow after blow, till men shall see
That Might and Right move hand in hand,
  And glorious must their triumph be.

THE GREAT BELL ROLAND.*

SUGGESTED BY THE PRESIDENT'S FIRST CALL FOR VOLUNTEERS.

BY THEODORE TILTON.

I.

TOLL! Roland, toll!
In old St. Bavon's tower,
At midnight hour,
The great Bell Roland spoke!
All souls that slept in Ghent awoke!
What meant the thunder stroke?
Why trembled wife and maid?
Why caught each man his blade?
Why echoed every street
With tramp of thronging feet?
All flying to the city's wall!
It was the warning call
That Freedom stood in peril of a foe!
And even timid hearts grew bold
Whenever Roland tolled,
And every hand a sword could hold!
So acted men

* The famous bell Roland, of Ghent, was an object of great affection to the people, because it rang to arm them when Liberty was in danger.

Like patriots then —
Three hundred years ago!

II.

Toll! Roland, toll!
Bell never yet was hung,
Between whose lips there swung
So grand a tongue!
If men be patriots still,
At thy first sound
True hearts will bound,
Great souls will thrill!
Then toll and strike the test
Through each man's breast,
Till loyal hearts shall stand confest, —
And may God's wrath smite all the rest!

III.

Toll! Roland, toll!
Not now in old St. Bavon's tower —
Not now at midnight hour —
Not now from River Scheldt to Zuyder Zee,
But here, — this side the sea! —
Toll here, in broad, bright day! —
For not by night awaits
A noble foe without the gates,
But perjured friends within betray,

And do the deed at noon!
Toll! Roland, toll!
Thy sound is not too soon!
To Arms! Ring out the Leader's call!
Reëcho it from East to West
Till every hero's breast
Shall swell beneath a soldier's crest!
Toll! Roland, toll!
Till cottager from cottage wall
Snatch pouch and powder-horn and gun!
The sire bequeathed them to the son
When only half their work was done!
Toll! Roland, toll!
Till swords from scabbards leap!
Toll! Roland, toll!
What tears can widows weep
Less bitter than when brave men fall!
Toll! Roland, toll!
In shadowed hut and hall
Shall lie the soldier's pall,
And hearts shall break while graves are [filled!
Amen! So God hath willed!
And may His grace anoint us all!

IV.

Toll! Roland, toll!
The Dragon on thy tower
Stands sentry to this hour,

And Freedom so stands safe in Ghent!
And merrier bells now ring,
And in the land's serene content
Men shout "God save the King!"
Until the skies are rent!
So let it be!
A kingly king is he
Who keeps his people free!
Toll! Roland, toll!
Ring out across the sea!
No longer They but We
Have now such need of thee!
Toll! Roland, toll!
Nor ever may thy throat
Keep dumb its warning note
Till Freedom's perils be outbraved!
Toll! Roland, toll!
Till Freedom's flag, wherever waved,
Shall shadow not a man enslaved!
Toll! Roland, toll!
From Northern lake to Southern strand!
Toll! Roland, toll!
Till friend and foe, at thy command,
Once more shall clasp each other's hand,
And shout, one-voiced, "God save the land!
And love the land that God hath saved!
Toll! Roland, toll!

April 16, 1861.

FORWARD!

BY REV. JOHN PIERPONT.

GOD, to the human soul,
And all the spheres that roll,
Wrapped by his Spirit in their robes of light,
Hath said: "The primal plan
Of all the world, and man,
Is Forward! Progress is your law — your right."

The despots of the earth,
Since Freedom had her birth,
Have to their subject nations said, "Stand still;"
So, from the Polar Bear,
Comes down the freezing air,
And stiffens all things with its deadly chill.

He who doth God resist —
God's old antagonist —
Would snap the chain that binds all things to him;
And in his godless pride,
All peoples would divide,
And scatter even the choirs of seraphim.

God, all the orbs that roll
Binds to one common goal —

One source of light and life — his radiant throne.
In one fraternal mind
All races would he bind,
Till every man in man a brother own.

Tyrants with tyrants league,
Corruption and intrigue
To strangle infant Liberty conspire.
Around her cradle, then,
Let self-devoted men
Gather, and keep unquenched her vital fire.

When Tyranny, grown bold,
To Freedom's host cries, "Hold!
Ye towards her temple at your peril march;"
"Stop," that great host replies,
Raising to heaven its eyes,
"Stop, first, the host that moves across yon arch!"

When Tyranny commands,
"Hold thou my victim's hands,
While I more firmly rivet on his chains,
Or with my bowie-knife,
I'll take your craven life,
Or show my streets bespattered with your brains."

Freedom, with forward tread,
Unblenching, turns her head,

And drawing from its sheath her flashing glave,
Calmly makes answer: "*Dare*
Touch of my head one hair,
I'll cut the cord that holds your every slave!"

THE PARTING.

I AM sitting, idly sitting, where the twilight shades are flitting,
And the memory of the past is drawing round me like a spell;
Breathes the last tones of the nearest, the fondest and the dearest,
Still within my ear in a tremulous farewell.

It is hard to think us parted — trusted, trusting, steel-true hearted —
And that many lengths may crumble from the lengthening chain of time,
Ere my lips may feel thy pressing, or my hair the light caressing
That have thrilled my heart with rapture, and a love almost sublime.

Ah, our lives have twined together like the vines in
sunny wreaths,
And we never thought to part till death should
break the chain
With which golden love had bound us, waving like
a halo round us
Every thought and every feeling, grasping joys,
ignoring pain.

Yet, thou 'rt gone! — thy country calls thee! Faction's
stormy cloud enthralls thee,
And I never more may look into the blue depths
of thine eyes, —
Never hear thy loud voice stealing, with its rich,
deep freight of feeling,
On my ear in gentle murmurs as the evening glory
dies.

Life seems 'reft of every beauty; I have scarce a
heart for duty,
As I sit here thinking, thinking of thee, darling,
far away.
Tears are falling fast and faster — Heaven grant
no dire disaster
May make the gloom eternal that is on my heart
to-day!

Yet, in all my pain and sorrow, could I call thee back to-morrow,
Dear, my lips should never breathe the words to hasten thy return :
Though I sit so sadly sobbing, with a heart so wildly throbbing,
I could never quench the sparks that on thy bosom's altar burn.

No! our hearts may wander darkling — still I see the diamond sparkling
Of the star that yet shall dawn to bid us hope for peace once more ;
And my soul leaps e'en in sadness, like an infant in its gladness,
To think how proud I 'll greet thee when the bloody strife is o'er.

I 'll not think of death and slaughter, tinged with blood the crystal water
Of the purling streams that murmur through the forests of our land,
But of banners proudly streaming where the camp-fires now are gleaming,
Hear the rallying shout of millions peal from Freedom's fearless band!

See I thee — bold, brave, and daring — on thy manly forehead wearing
The shadow of a purpose strong as every pulse of life,
See thee strike the foe before thee, while the rolling clouds sweep o'er thee —
Oh! 'mid clashing swords and sabres, in the hottest of the strife.

I would never have thee falter! — better death or felon's halter
Than to see our cause defeated and a nation bowed in shame.
Were I man, grim death should claim me ere a coward's thought should shame me,
Or the stigma of inaction rise upon my manhood's fame!

Leave — God have thee in His keeping ever, waking or in sleeping;
Every hour I breathe a prayer for our country's cause and thee;
And I feel this love will fold thee, till mine eyes again behold thee
In the flush of manly beauty and the pride of victory!

B. Z. S.

THE SOLDIER'S "GOOD-BY."

BY MARY E. NEALY.

GOOD-BY, my wife, my child, my friend,
'T is hard to leave you all;
But there 's a God in heaven above
Will bless and shield you with His love,
If I am doomed to fall.

You know I could not stay, dear love,
When over all the land
The shot of Sumter circled round,
And lifted, at a single bound,
This mighty patriot-band.

A thrill that never else had swept
Across this soul of mine,
Stirred up each tingling drop of blood,
Ready to pour a votive flood
Upon my country's shrine.

O dearest! there 's a manhood lies,
Deep in these slender forms,
We know not of, till in our skies
Such clouds of danger o'er us rise
To fill our land with storms.

Then, like a mountain stream it comes,
    A stream of power and might;
It echoes to the beat of drums,
It quails not when the fiery bombs
    Break fiercely on the sight.

This war is sad; but I thank God
    For this one blessed taste
Of manhood, strong within my blood;—
Of strength unknown, a mighty flood
    Which else had gone to waste.

My arms seem braced with nerves of steel,
    My soul is firm and strong;
And, dearest, even now I feel
The power to crush beneath my heel
    My share of this foul wrong.

The man who springs not to his sword
    In such a time as this,
To see his country's fame restored,
Is weak as he who slew his Lord
    With a deceitful kiss.

Then ask me not. I cannot stay,
    My own, my blessed wife;
The God that looks on us to-day

Will listen to you when you pray,
And shield your soldier's life.

Yet if I come not back again,
But fall beside my foe,
This blood will not be spilled in vain
Though it should fall like crimson rain
Where crimson waters flow.

I'm strong enough to die, dear love,
In such a cause as ours;
For I shall see from Heaven above
Freedom's fair bow above *you wave*,
Entwined with Freedom's flowers.

Now kiss me one "good-by," my wife,
Your task is worse than mine;
For while I revel in the strife,
You can but pray for this poor life,
With heroism divine.

'T is weary — all the dark suspense
A woman has to bear:
The anguished thoughts, the woe intense,
While booming cannon bear her hence
A fear for every prayer.

But you — you must be strong and bright;
  You are a soldier's wife :
I 'll think of you by day and night,
Your love shall nerve me in the fight;
  Good-by, my love, my life!

Louisville, Ky.

THE WOODS OF TENNESSEE.

ANONYMOUS.

THE whip-poor-will is calling
  From its perch on the splintered limb,
And the plaintive notes are echoing
  Through the aisles of the forest dim :
The slanting threads of starlight
  Are silvering shrub and tree,
And the spot where the loved are sleeping,
  In the woods of Tennessee.

The leaves are gently rustling,
  But they 're stained with a tinge of red —
For they proved to many a soldier
  Their last and lonely bed.
As they prayed in mortal agony
  To God to set them free,

Death touched them with his finger,
  In the woods of Tennessee.

In the list of the killed and wounded,
  Ah, me! alas! we saw
The name of our noble brother,
  Who went to the Southern war.
He fell in the tide of battle
  On the banks of the old "Hatchie,"
And rests 'neath the wild grape arbors
  In the woods of Tennessee.

There 's many still forms lying
  In their forgotten graves,
On the green slope of the hill-sides
  Along Potomac's waves;
But the memory will be ever sweet
  Of him so dear to me,
On his country's altar offered,
  In the woods of Tennessee.

A CALL TO THE BRAVE.

UP, up ye sons of freedom! born
  Beneath our nation's God-blest sky,

God and our country call you forth
  To fight, to conquer, or to die.
Shall our fair land, by heaven so blest,
  Become a tyrant monarch's throne?
Shall thy God's altars desecrate —
  Around whose shrines our hearts have grown?

Shall they, beneath a grinding heel,
  Tread down our brave and noble men?
Shall they, with despot's iron rule,
  Make of our land a demon's den?
Shall prayers and tears and sighs and groans
  Move Heaven's great listening heart to tears,
While ye sit still with folded hands
  Nursing a coward's craven fears?

Shall our forefathers from their graves
  Rise up to see the traitor tread
Over their blood-bought resting-place? —
  Over their blood-stained coffin-bed?
Shall they rise up to taunt ye now
  In this our nation's peril hour?
Shall God look down and see his courts
  Degraded by a tyrant's power?

Ah, no! thank God, you see your place!
  You *do* your duty for the right!

Brave hearts, ye have our truest prayers
  That God may help you in His might.
You have our prayers, you have our tears,
  You have our truest sympathy:—
God shield and guard and bless you all,
  In this your fight for liberty.

Though life may falter when we part
  With brother, father, husband, friend,
That God above who reads each heart
  Shall find us with you to the end;
Be brave, and in the battle's din,
  Amid the smoke of muskets bright,
Keep in each heart this cheering thought,—
  We *pray* for you both *day* and *night*.

Louisville, Ky.

THE VOLUNTEER'S WIFE TO HER HUSBAND

DON'T stop a moment to think, John,
  Your country calls — then go;
Don't think of me or the children, John,
  I'll care for them, you know.
Leave the corn upon the stalks, John,
  Potatoes on the hill,

And the pumpkins on the vines, John —
  I 'll gather them with a will.
But take your gun and go, John,
  Take your gun and go,
For Ruth can drive the oxen, John,
  And I can use the hoe.

I 've heard my grandsire tell, John,
  (He fought at Bunker Hill,)
How he counted all his life and wealth
  His country's offering still.
Shall we shame the brave old blood, John,
  That flowed on Monmouth Plain ?
No ! take your gun and go, John,
  If you ne 'er return again.
Then take your gun and go, etc.

Our army 's short of blankets, John,
  Then take this heavy pair ;
I spun and wove them when a girl,
  And worked them with great care.
There 's a rose in every corner, John,
  And there 's my name, you see ;
On the cold ground they 'll warmer feel
  That they were made by me.
Then take your gun and go, etc.

And if it be God's will, John,
  You ne'er come back again,
I'll do my best for the children, John,
  In sorrow, want, and pain.
In winter nights I'll teach them all
  That I have learned at school,
To love the country, keep the laws,
  Obey the Saviour's rule.
Then take your gun and go, etc.

And in the village church, John,
  And at our humble board,
We'll pray that God will keep you, John,
  And heavenly aid afford;
And all who love their country's cause
  Will love and bless you too,
And nights and mornings they will pray
  For Freedom and for you.
Then take your gun and go, etc.

And now good-by to you, John —
  I cannot say farewell;
We'll hope and pray for the best, John;
  God's goodness none can tell.
Be His great arm around you, John,
  To guard you night and day;

Be our beloved country's shield,
  Till the war has passed away.
Then take your gun and go, etc.

OUR COUNTRY IS CALLING.

BY F. H. HEDGE, D. D.

[*Wohl auf! Cameraden! aufs Pferd, aufs Pferd!*]

OUR country is calling! Go forth! go forth!
  To danger and glory, ye gallants!
In danger your manhood must prove its worth,
  There hearts are weighed in the balance;
And he who would win his life at last
Must throw it all on the battle's cast.

Our country is calling, our country that bleeds
  With daggers which Treason has planted;
'T is Honor that beckons where Loyalty leads,
  We follow with spirits undaunted.
The soldier who fronts death face to face
Is foremost now of the patriot race.

Our country is calling! we come! we come!
  For Freedom and Union we rally;

Our heart-beat echoes the beating drum,
  Our thoughts with the trumpet tally;
Each bosom pants for the doomful day
When the rebels shall meet us in battle array.

Our country is calling with names that of old
  Emblazoned America's story;
May those of to-day, when its tale shall be told,
  Blaze with them forever in glory!
Be our banner redeemed the reward of our scars,
No scathe on its stripes and no cloud on its stars!

THE VOICE OF THE NORTH.

BY JOHN G. WHITTIER.

UP the hill-side, down the glen,
  Rouse the sleeping citizen:
Summon out the might of men!

Like a lion growling low —
Like a night-storm rising slow —
Like the tread of unseen foe —

It is coming — it is nigh!
Stand your homes and altars by,
On your own free threshold die.

Clang the bells in all your spires,
On the gray hills of your sires
Fling to heaven your signal-fires.

Oh! for God and duty stand,
Heart to heart and hand to hand,
Round the old graves of the land.

Whoso shrinks or falters now,
Whoso to the yoke would bow,
Brand the craven on his brow.

Freedom's soil has only place
For a free and fearless race —
None for traitors false and base.

Perish party — perish clan;
Strike together while you can,
Like the strong arm of one man.

Like the angels' voice sublime,
Heard above a world of crime,
Crying for the end of Time.

With one heart and with one mouth,
Let the North speak to the South;
Speak the word befitting both.

ON GUARD.

BY JOHN G. NICOLAY.

IN the black terror-night,
  On yon mist-shrouded hill,
Slowly, with footstep light,
  Stealthy and grim and still,
Like ghost in winding sheet
  Risen at midnight bell,
Over his lonely beat
  Marches the sentinel!

In storm-defying cloak —
  Hand on his trusty gun —
Heart, like a heart of oak —
  Eye, never-setting sun;
Speaks but the challenge-shout,
  All foes without the line,
Heeds but, to solve the doubt,
  Watchword and countersign.

Camp-ward, the watchfires gleam
  Beacon-like in the gloom;
Round them his comrades dream
  Pictures of youth and home.
While in his heart the bright
  Hope-fires shine everywhere,

In love's enchanting light
  Memory lies dreaming there.

Faint, through the silence come
  From the foes' grim array,
Growl of impatient drum
  Eager for morrow's fray;
Echo of song and shout,
  Curse and carousal glee,
As in a fiendish rout
  Demons at revelry.

Close, in the gloomy shade —
  Danger lurks ever nigh —
Grasping his dagger-blade
  Crouches th' assassin spy;
Shrinks at the guardsman's tread,
  Quails 'fore his gleaming eyes,
Creeps back with baffled hate,
  Cursing his cowardice.

Naught can beguile his bold,
  Unsleeping vigilance;
E'en in the fireflame, old
  Visions unheeded dance.
Fearless of lurking spy,
  Scornful of wassail-swell,

With an undaunted eye
  Marches the sentinel.

Low, to his trusty gun
  Eagerly whispers he,
"Wait, with the morning sun
  March we to victory.
Fools, into Satan's clutch
  Leaping ere dawn of day:
He who would fight must watch,
  He who would win must pray."

Pray! for the night hath wings;
  Watch! for the foe is near;
March! till the morning brings
  Fame-wreath or soldier's bier.
So shall the poet write,
  When all hath ended well,
"Thus through the nation's night
  Marched Freedom's sentinel."

THE CAVALRY CHARGE.

BY FRANCIS A. DURIVAGE.

WITH bray of the trumpet
  And roll of the drum,

And keen ring of bugle,
  The cavalry come.
Sharp clank the steel scabbards,
  The bridle-chains ring,
And foam from red nostrils
  The wild chargers fling.

Tramp ! tramp ! o'er the greensward
  That quivers below,
Scarce held by the curb-bit
  The fierce horses go !
And the grim-visaged colonel,
  With ear-rending shout,
Peals forth to the squadrons
  The order — " Trot out ! "

One hand on the sabre,
  And one on the rein,
The troopers move forward
  In line on the plain.
As rings the word " Gallop ! "
  The steel scabbards clank,
And each rowel is pressed
  To a horse's hot flank :
And swift is their rush
  As the wild torrent's flow,
When it pours from the crag
  On the valley below.

"Charge!" thunders the leader:
  Like shaft from the bow
Each mad horse is hurled
  On the wavering foe.
A thousand bright sabres
  Are gleaming in air;
A thousand dark horses
  Are dashed on the square.

Resistless and reckless
  Of aught may betide,
Like demons, not mortals,
  The wild troopers ride.
Cut right! and cut left!—
  For the parry who needs?
The bayonets shiver
  Like wind-shattered reeds.
Vain — vain the red volley
  That bursts from the square,—
The random-shot bullets
  Are wasted in air.
Triumphant, remorseless,
  Unerring as death,—
No sabre that's stainless
  Returns to its sheath.

The wounds that are dealt
  By that murderous steel

Will never yield case
  For the surgeon to heal.
Hurrah! they are broken —
  Hurrah! boys, they fly —
None linger save those
  Who but linger to die.

Rein up your hot horses
  And call in your men, —
The trumpet sounds "Rally
  To color" again.
Some saddles are empty,
  Some comrades are slain,
And some noble horses
  Lie stark on the plain,
But war 's a chance game, boys,
  And weeping is vain.

SNOW SCULPTURE.

BY GEORGE W. BUNGAY.

ON hills and forests bare and brown,
I see the silent snow come down,
  So soft and white,

Like showers of blossoms winds have blown
From flowers of light.

Faster and faster fall the flakes,
On the dim woods and silver lakes,
From stormy skies,
Like soft words on a heart that breaks
When pity sighs.

Ye wailing winds that sadly sigh,
Above the graves where heroes lie,
In sorrow blow,
And build white columns, broad and high,
Of stainless snow.

Let pyramids of spotless hue
Point to the bending arch of blue
Without a stain,
And mark the place where sleep the true,
In battle slain.

Ye unseen sculptors in the air,
Go carve designs in beauty there,
And grave the name
Of BAKER, deep in letters fair
As wreaths of fame.

Go where the bending willow weeps
Over the tomb where ELLSWORTH sleeps,
And softly write
The epitaph that history keeps
In letters white.

Quarry from clouds a shaft to tower
Above the spot where sleeps the flower
Of armies true,
'Till blossoms rise in sun and shower,
Red, white, and blue.

SOLDIER'S MORNING SONG.

Erhebt euch von der Erde.

YE sleepers, hear the warning,
Lift up your drowsy heads!
Loud snort the steeds "Good-morning!"
Forsake your grassy beds.
The sun-lit steel is gleaming,
Undimmed by battle's breath;
Of garlands men are dreaming,
And thinking, too, of death.

Thou gracious God! in kindness
  Look down from thy blue tent:
We rushed not forth in blindness,
  By Thee to battle sent.
O lift on high before us
  Thy truth's all-conquering sign:
The flag of Christ floats o'er us,
  The fight, O Lord, is thine!

There yet shall come a morning, —
  A morning mild and bright;
All good men bless its dawning,
  And angels hail the sight.
Soon from her night of sadness
  This suffering land shall wake:
O break, thou day of gladness!
  Thou day of Freedom break!

Then peals from all the towers!
  And peals from every breast!
And peace from stormy hours,
  And love and joy and rest!
Then songs of triumph loudly
  Shall swell through all the air,
And we 'll remember proudly,
  We, too, brave blades! were there.

C. T. Brooks.

AFTER THE BATTLE.

BY E. L. R.

THE cannon's thunders ceased to swell —
The whistling shot and shrieking shell
No more with vengeful fury sped
Amid the mangled and the dead.

A sullen silence broods around —
For on that dark and bloody ground
The gallant champions of the Free,
Fought, bled, and died for Liberty!

Perchance a brother's fate was sealed,
Upon that solemn battle-field;
And, e'en while in the arms of Death,
A prayer for home — his latest breath!

Where raged the fury of the fray
Two warriors, — side by side they lay, —
All rent with many a ghastly wound,
Their life-blood bathed the crimson ground.

Fierce foes in life — the cannon's roar
Will rouse their bitter ire no more;
They perished in a dread embrace,
With eye to eye, and face to face.

The war-steed wanders o'er the plain,
Seeking amid the heaps of slain
The form of him, whose hand would guide
His courser through the battle-tide.

The chieftain's sword, grasped in his hand,
Still seemed to beckon on his band;
He fell — while rose the joyous cry,
The mighty shout of victory.

Close by yon straggling mass of wall,
A youth was seen to reel and fall,
Where fiercest lead and iron rained —
His purple gore his colors stained.

With dying shout he partly rose,
And waved the banner at his foes;
Then strained it to his bloody breast,
Smiled a glad smile and sunk to rest.

O, piteous sight! Yet Freedom gave
A Hero's shroud, a Martyr's grave
To the loved ones, whose blood shall rise
To Heaven, a holy sacrifice.

Their noble deeds of valor done,
A Patriot's name, immortal, won!

And on our hearts will e'er remain
The memory of the gallant slain.

A nation's tears will greet the dead,
Whose blood for Freedom's cause was shed;
Her blessings greet the brave, who passed
Safe from the fury of the blast.

A MOTHER WAITING FOR THE NEWS.

BY DAVID M. MENAMIN.

HOW wearily the hours pass
  Since, through the ambient air,
The lightnings flashed the startling fact,
  A battle has been there, —
There, where my noble, honest boy
  The path of fame pursues;
But, ah! my aching heart will burst,
  While waiting for the news.

Wounded upon that gory field,
  Forsaken he may die;
Nor mother there to wet his lips,
  Nor raise his hopes on high;

Disfigured, stained, his features marred
  By many a scar and bruise;
Ah! who can tell what mothers feel
  While waiting for the news.

Ye wise men who have made this war
  To make all mankind free,
Oh! know you not this boy of mine
  Was all the world to me?
If he is gone, what have I left —
  What comfort can I choose?
A mother's heart condemns your deeds,
  While waiting for the news!

If I am wrong, O God! forgive
  This throbbing heart and brain,
But who can justify their aims
  If my poor boy is slain?
Yet they, whose sons are safe at home,
  May take far different views,
And cry aloud, "More blood! more blood!"
  O God! send me good news.

HE SLEEPS WHERE HE FELL.

ANONYMOUS.

HE sleeps where he fell 'mid the battle's roar,
  With his comrades true and brave;
And his noble form we shall see no more, —
  It rests in a hero's grave:
Where the rebel foe in his might came forth,
  With all his power and pride;
And our gallant men from the rugged North
  Like patriots fought and died.

He sleeps near the hill where bright flowers grow,
  In the wildest woodland shade;
Where the valley stream, in the dell below,
  With an echo fills the glade;
Where the boasting lines of the traitor-South
  Filed up, o'er the grassy banks,
Till the bursting shells from our cannon's mouth
  Flung death in their broken ranks.

He sleeps 'neath the sod where I prayerfully knelt,
  While the enemy round me stood,
As I took from the corse his battle-belt,
  Still wet with his heart's warm blood;
And the summer day closed its light on earth,
  And my soul grew sad with pain,

As they bore me away with oaths and mirth,
  O'er piles of the bleeding slain.

He sleeps where the blest of our glorious dead
  Were left on the sacred land;
Where the daring deeds, ere his spirit fled,
  He led with a bold command!
He sleeps — yes, he sleeps, undisturbed by war,
  Though tyrants tramp o'er his breast;
For, with those who slumber in glory afar,
  He takes an immortal rest.

Fort Delaware.

THE RED STAIN ON THE LEAVES.

BY G. W. BUNGAY.

THE wood-bird's nest upon the bough
  Deserted hangs, and heaped with leaves;
Once filled with life and joy, but now
  Sad as a stricken heart that grieves.
Amid the light of such a scene,
  Where silent vales and hills are clad
In gayest hues of gold and green,
  Why should the human heart be sad?

Yet sombre thoughts flit through the mind,
  And pass unspoken and unsung,
As leaves, touched by the autumn wind,
  Fall from the twigs to which they clung.
Here, like the patriarch in his dream,
  We see the ladder angels trod;
The mountains to our vision seem
  A footstool at the throne of God.

The veils of golden mist that rise
  Over the woodlands to the sea,
Drop where the gallant soldier lies,
  Whose furlough is eternity.
Upon the leaves now sear and red,
  That once were flakes of fire to me,
I see the blood our armies shed,
  That our dear country may be free.

THE SOLDIER'S MOTHER.

ANONYMOUS.

IT is night; almost morning — the clock has
  struck three;

Who can tell where, this moment, my darling may
be!
On the window has gathered the moisture like
dew;
I can see where the moonbeams steal tremblingly
through;
It is cold, but not windy, — how dreary and damp
It must be for our soldiers exposed in the camp!
Though I know it is warmer and balmier there,
Yet I shrink from the thought of the chilling night-
air;
For he never was used to the hardships of men
When at home, for I shielded and cherished him
then;
And to all that could tend to his comfort I saw, —
For he seemed like a child till he went to the
War!

He is twenty, I know; and boys younger than he,
In the ranks going by, every day we can see;
And those stronger and prouder, by far I have
met,
But I never have seen a young soldier, as yet,
With so gallant a mien, or so lofty a brow, —
How the sun and the wind must have darkened it
now!
How he will have been changed when he comes
from the South! —

With his beard shutting out the sweet smiles of his
 mouth;
And the tremulous beauty, the womanly grace,
Will be bronzed from the delicate lines of his face,
Where, of late, only childhood's soft beauty I saw,—
For he seemed like a child till he went to the
 War!

He was always so gentle, and ready to yield;
And so frank, there was nothing kept back or con-
 cealed;
He was always so sparkling with laughter and joy,
I had thought he never could cease being a boy;
But when sounded the cannon for battle, and when
Rose the rallying cry of our Nation for men,
From the dream-loving mood of his boyhood he
 passed;
From his path the light fetters of pleasure he cast;
And rose, ready to stand in the perilous van,
Not the tremulous boy, but the resolute man;
And I gazed on him sadly, with trembling and
 awe,—
He was only a child till he went to the War!

There are homes that are humbler and sadder than
 ours;
There are ways that are barer of beauty and
 flowers;

There are those that must suffer for fire and bread,
Living only to sorrow and wish they were dead;
I must try and be patient — I must not repine —
But what heart is more lonely, more anxious than
mine!
Or what hearth can be darker than mine seems
to be,
Now the glow of the firelight is all I can see, —
Where my darling, in beauty, so lately I saw, —
He was only a child, till he went to the War!

THE DEAD DRUMMER-BOY.

'MIDST tangled roots that lined the wild ravine
Where the fierce fight raged hottest through
the day,
And where the dead in scattered heaps were seen,
Amid the darkling forest's shade and sheen,
Speechless in death he lay.

The setting sun, which glanced athwart the place
In slanting lines, like amber-tinted rain,
Fell sidewise on the drummer's upturned face,
Where death had left his gory finger's trace
In one bright crimson stain.

The silken fringes of his once bright eye
  Lay like a shadow on his cheek so fair;
His lips were parted by a long-drawn sigh,
That with his soul had mounted to the sky
    On some wild martial air.

No more his hand the fierce tattoo shall beat,
  The shrill reveille, or the long roll's call,
Or sound the charge, when in the smoke and heat
Of fiery onset, foe with foe shall meet,
    And gallant men shall fall.

Yet may be in some happy home, that one,
  A mother, reading from the list of dead,
Shall chance to view the name of her dear son,
And move her lips to say, " God's will be done ! "
    And bow in grief her head.

But more than this what tongue shall tell his story ?
  Perhaps his boyish longings were for fame ;
He lived, he died ; and so, *memento mori*, —
Enough if on the page of War and Glory
    Some hand has writ his name.

A NATIONAL HYMN.

BY PARK BENJAMIN.

GREAT God! to whom our nation's woes,
Our dire distress, our angry foes,
In all their awful gloom are known,
We bow to Thee and Thee alone.

We pray Thee mitigate this strife,
Attended by such waste of life,
Such wounds and anguish, groans and tears,
That fill our inmost hearts with fears.

Oh, darkly now the tempest rolls,
Wide o'er our desolated souls;
Yet, beaten downward to the dust,
In Thy forgiveness still we trust.

We trust to Thy protecting power
In this, our country's saddest hour,
And pray that Thou wilt spread Thy shield
Above us in the camp and field.

O, God of battles! let Thy might
Protect our armies in the fight —
'Till they shall win the victory,
And set the hapless bondmen free.

'Till, guided by Thy glorious hand,
Those armies reunite the land,
And North and South alike shall raise
To God their peaceful hymns of praise.

AVENGED!

BY ORPHEUS C. KERR.*

GOD'S scales of Justice hang between
The deed Unjust and the end Unseen,
And the sparrow's fall in the one is weighed
By the Lord's own hand in the other laid.

In the prairie path to our Sunset gate,
In the flow'ring heart of a new-born State,
Are the hopes of an old man's waning years,
'Neath headstones worn with an old man's tears.

When the bright sun sinks in the rose-lipped West,
His last red ray is the headstone's crest:
And the mounds he laves in a crimson flood
Are a Soldier's wealth baptized in blood!

Do ye ask who reared those headstones there,
And crowned with thorns a sire's gray hair?

* *R. H. Newell.*

And by whom the Land's great debt was paid
To the Soldier old, in the graves they made?

Shrink, Pity, shrink, at the question dire;
And, Honor, burn in a blush of fire!
Turn, Angel, turn, from the page thine eyes,
Or the Sin, once written, never dies!

They were men of the land he had fought to save
From a foreign foe that had crossed the wave,
When his sunlit youth was a martial song,
And shook a throne as it swelled along.

They were sons of a clime whose soft, warm breath
Is the soul of earth, and a life in death;
Where the Summer dreams on the couch of Spring,
And songs of birds through the whole year ring;

Where the falling leaf is the cup that grew
To catch the gems of the new leaf's dew,
And the winds that through the vine-leaves creep
Are the sighs of Time in a pleasant sleep.

But there lurked a taint in the clime so blest,
Like a serpent coiled in a ringdove's nest,
And the human sounds to the ear it gave
Were the clank of chains on a low-browed Slave.

The Soldier old, at his sentry-post,
Where the sun's last trail of light is lost,
Beheld the shame of the land he loved,
And the old, old love in his bosom moved.

He cried to the land, Beware! Beware
Of the symboled curse in the Bondman there!
And a prophet's soul in fire came down
To live in the voice of old John Brown.

He cried; and the ingrate answer came
In words of steel from a tongue of flame;
They dyed his hearth in the blood of kin,
And his dear ones fell for the Nation's Sin!

Oh, matchless deed! that a fiend might scorn;
Oh, deed of shame! for a world to mourn;
A prophet's pay in his blood most dear,
And a land to mock at a Father's tear!

Is 't strange that the tranquil soul of age
Was turned to strife in a madman's rage?
Is 't strange that the cry of blood did seem
Like the roll of drums in a martial dream?

Is 't strange that the clank of the Helot's chain
Should drive the Wrong to the old man's brain,

To fire his heart with a Santon's zeal,
And mate his arm to the Soldier's steel?

The bane of Wrong to its depth had gone,
And the sword of Right from its sheath was drawn,
But the cabined Slave heard not his cry,
And the old man armed him but to die.

Ye may call him mad that he did not quail
When his stout blade broke on the unblest mail;
Ye may call him mad, that he struck alone,
And made the land's dark Curse his own;

But the Eye of God looked down and saw
A just life lost by an unjust law;
And black was the day with God's own frown
When the Southern Cross was a martyr's Crown!

Apostate clime! the blood then shed
Fell thick with vengeance on thy head,
To weigh it down 'neath the coming rod,
When thy red hand should be stretched to God.

Behold the price of the life ye took;
At the death ye gave 't was a world that shook:
And the despot deed that one heart broke,
From their slavish sleep a million woke!

Not all alone did the victim fall,
Whose wrongs first brought him to your thrall:
The old man played a Nation's part,
And ye struck your blow at the Nation's heart!

The freemen host is at your door,
And a voice goes forth with a stern "No more!"
To the deadly Curse, whose swift redeem
Was the visioned thought of John Brown's dream.

To the Country's Wrong and the Country's Stain,
It shall prove as the scythe to the yielding grain;
And the dauntless power to spread it forth
Is the freeborn soul of the chainless North.

From the East and West and North they come,
To the bugle's call and the roll of drum;
And a form walks viewless by their side, —
A form that was born when the Old Man died!

The Soldier old in his grave may rest,
Afar with his dead in the prairie West;
But the red ray falls on the headstone there,
Like a God's reply to a Soldier's prayer.

He may sleep in peace 'neath the greenwood pall,
For the land's great heart hath heard his call;

And a people's Will and a people's Might
Shall right the Wrong and proclaim the Right.

The foe may howl at the fiat just,
And gnash his fangs in the trodden dust;
But the battle leaves his bark a wreck,
And the Freeman's heel is on his track.

Not all in vain is the lesson taught,
That a great soul's Dream is the world's New
Thought;
And the Scaffold marked with a death sublime
Is the Throne ordained for the coming time.

FLAG OF THE CONSTELLATION.

BY T. BUCHANAN READ.

THE stars of morn on our banner borne
With the iris of heaven are blended;
The hand of our sires first mingled those fires,
And by us they shall be defended.

CHORUS.

Then hail the true Red, White, and Blue,
The flag of the constellation;

It sails as it sailed by our forefathers hailed,
  O'er battles that made us a nation.

What hand so bold, as strike from its fold,
  One star or one stripe of its bright'ning?
For him be those stars each a fiery Mars,
  Each stripe be a terrible lightning.
    Then hail the true Red, etc.

Its meteor form shall ride the storm,
  Till the fiercest of foes surrender;
The storm gone by, it shall gild the sky,
  A rainbow of peace and of splendor.
    Then hail the true Red, etc.

Peace to the world, is our motto unfurled,
  Though we shun not the field that is gory;
At home or abroad, fearing none but our God,
  We will carve our own pathway to glory.
    Then hail the true Red, etc.

WAR SONG.

BY WILLIAM H. C. HOSMER.

WITH sword on thigh, "to do or die,"
  I march to meet the foe;

A pirate band have cursed the land,
  Then deal the deadly blow.
To Richmond on, and write upon
  Her walls the words of doom;
Secession's horde from Freedom's sword
  Deserves a bloody tomb.

Sound, bugle, sound! a rally round
  The Star-flag of the Free;
Nursed by a flood of generous blood
  Was Freedom's sacred tree.
Accursed by God in dust be trod
  Rebellion's hellish horde;
The fiends to tame hearts are aflame
  With cannon-peal and sword.

'T is hard to leave the babes that grieve
  For a fond, absent sire;
His cherished wife, charm of his life,
  To brave the battle's fire;
But duty calls, and loudly falls
  Our war-cry on the ear;
Our banners wave above the brave —
  Then on! and know not fear.

THE FLAG OF THE SKY.

ANONYMOUS.

WILLIE stood at the window, —
  Little Willie of five years old, —
Watching the rainbow colors,
  As they fade in the sunset's gold.

Red pennants and streamers of fire,
  On the blue expanse unfurl,
And over the red the white clouds lie,
  Like floating mists of pearl.

"Is n't it beautiful, mamma?
  And the dark eyes grow so bright,
They almost seem to catch the glow
  Of the sky's wild glory light.

"See, there is the red, mamma,
  And there is the beautiful blue;
Did God make the beautiful red,
  And did he make the white clouds, too?

"And away up, up in the sky,
  Is such a little bright star;
Why, God is for the Union, —
  Is n't He, mamma?"

TO-DAY.

BY JOEL BENTON.

THROUGH gates of gold and pearl he came,
The eastern hills were all aflame;

He touched the earth with tender light,
And kissed away the shades of night.

"Here comes our Friend," the Lily said;
The Rose blushed to a deeper red,

And all the gentle race of flowers
Poured incense for the Morning Hours.

The sky bent down its deepest blue;
From tree to tree the Robins flew;

The jewelled fields grew hourly fair;
Bird-carols floated on the air; —

The woods were still, as in a dream,
And like a diamond shone the stream

"To-day, a King is, in disguise,"
Observed the poet, shrewdly wise;

A servant, also, to obey
And lead you where you point the way.

Who wrestle with him hour by hour,
He leads to Fame and Wealth and Power;

For, who win his treasured stores,
Must first assail his realm by Force.

Small note he takes of varying creeds,
His record lies in words and deeds; —

Actions that grow to fair renown, —
These are the jewels in his crown.

Discourse is vain; his lips are dumb,
No oracles from him can come; —

To all the questioner says or thinks,
He is as subtle as the Sphinx.

In him all issues centred are,
His realm extends to Sun and Star, —

And on his car, which will not wait,
He bears the Keys of Time and Fate.

Up, Man! and labor while you may;
Behold your King, or Slave, TO-DAY.

FOLLOWING THE DRUM.

"KISS me good-by, my dear!" he said;
"When I come back we will be wed."
Crying, she kissed him, "Good-by, Ned!"
And the soldier followed the drum,
The drum,
The echoing, echoing drum.

Rataplan! Rataplan! Rataplan!
Follow me, follow me, each true man;
Living or dying, strike while you can!
And the soldiers followed the drum,
The drum,
The echoing, echoing drum.

Proudly and firmly marched off the men;
Who had a sweetheart thought of her then;
Tears were coming, but brave lips smiled when
The soldiers followed the drum,
The drum,
The echoing, echoing drum.

One with a woman's curl next to his heart,
He felt her last smile pierce like a dart;
She thought "death in life" comes when we part
  From soldiers following the drum,
        The drum,
  The echoing, echoing drum.

THE UNION!

A NATIONAL SONG.

BY FRANCIS DE HAES JANVIER.

"Liberty and Union, now and forever, one and inseparable!"
WEBSTER.

I.

THE Union! The Union! The hope of the
    free!
  Howsoe'er we may differ, in this we agree:—
Our glorious banner no traitor shall mar,
  By effacing a stripe, or destroying a star!
Division! No, never! The Union forever!
  And cursed be the hand that our country would
    sever!

II.

The Union! The Union! 'T was purchased with
blood!
Side by side, to secure it, our forefathers stood: —
From the North to the South, through the length
of the land,
Ran the war-cry which summoned that patriot
band!
Division! No, never! The Union forever!
And cursed be the hand that our country would
sever!

III

The Union! The Union! At Lexington first,
Through the clouds of oppression, its radiance
burst: —
But at Yorktown rolled back the last vapory crest,
And, a bright constellation, it blazed in the
West!
Division! No, never! The Union forever!
And cursed be the hand that our country would
sever!

IV.

The Union! The Union! Its heavenly light
Cheers the hearts of the nations who grope in
the night, —

And, athwart the wide ocean, falls, gilding the
tides,
A path to the country where Freedom abides!
Division! No, never! The Union forever!
And cursed be the hand that our country would
sever!

V.

The Union! The Union! In God we repose!
We confide in the power that vanquished our
foes!
The God of our fathers, — Oh, still may He be
The strength of the Union, the hope of the free!
Division! No, never! The Union forever!
And cursed be the hand that our country would
sever!

THE BATTLE.

BY RUTH N. CROMWELL.

THE battle was over, we had won it, they said;
I heard the brief tale of the heroes who led,—
Of the hosts that went in, of the few that came out,
Of the charge for the Union, — the carnage and
rout.

God pity the hearts that are cleft to the core
For the heroes who fell on Potomac's blue shore!

Alone by my casement, at the dead of the night,
Like a blast from the battle came news of the fight;
I heard not the shriek of the death-dooming gun,
I saw not the sabres that flashed in the sun;
No tumult of glory lit up the dark plain
Whose furrows ran red with the blood of the slain.

Oh, deaf was my ear to the whoop and the roar,
And blind was my eye to the trappings of war;
I saw not the charger, decked out in his pride,
For the pale horse of Death that stalked by his side;
O pæans of joy, hosanna and prayer,
Ye were lost in the dirges that burdened the air.

Ay, naught but the wail from mountain and strand,
That arose to the skies from the heart of the land;
O Columbia, my country, proud land of my birth,
I have need to remember thy mission on earth;
I have need to remember, heart-weary and torn,
The flag that our fathers unfurl'd to the morn.

May the sheen of thy rifles die out in the glade,
With brother no longer 'gainst brother arrayed;
May the swords of the children be sheathed to the
hilt
On the plain where the blood of the martyrs was
spilt;
May the Star-Spangled Banner, bright gleaming
of heaven,
Float over the hearts that no longer are riven.

Thou art travailing to-day, in anguish and woe, —
The breast that should shield is the breast of thy
foe;
While I gaze on thy hills, where naught should be
seen
But the low-waving lines of thy emerald green,
I have need to remember, all memories above,
That the God whom we worship chastiseth in love.

THE DYING SOLDIER.

WEARY and worn to a skeleton form
He lay on a couch of pain,
And his wish at even, his prayer at morn,
Were to visit his home again.

He talked of his mother far away,
  And he talked of his lonely wife,
When the fever frenzied his burning head
  And loosened his hold of life.

He talked of his home, the fair free land,
  The home of his childhood's play ;
He talked of his babe, and the large tears fell
  And rolled from his cheeks away.

We told him his feet might never again
  Walk over his native sod,
But ere long they should tread the golden streets,
  At home in the city of God.

And we said though his eye should never behold
  The forms of his earth's deep love,
He should wait for them there, by the life river fair,
  In the garden of beauty above.

But he wept, and he talked of his burial lone
  In a stranger's unnoticed bed, —
That no rose by affection's hand would be trained
  To wave o'er his grave when dead.

We told him that God would mark the spot
  Where all of his children lay,

And not one of his loved ones be forgot
  On the resurrection day.

But he sighed, and whispered — " So long, so long,
  So many long weary years!
And my lonely wife and little one
  Alone in a vale of tears."

We told him the Word of God had gone forth,
  In truth and holiness,
As the Friend of the widow's lonely life,
  The Guide of the fatherless.

When death had stilled that loving heart,
  Kind hands with gentle care
Had saved for her, that lonely wife,
  One tress of his long, bright hair.

Then they wrapped the worn-out soldier's clothes
  Round the martyred hero's breast,
And in his rude, unvarnished bed,
  Laid him sadly away to rest.

Not a hymn was sung, not a prayer was raised,
  Not a word of counsel said,
But the hireling's rude, uncareful hands
  Piled the damp mould o'er his head. M.

HEAD OF THE COLUMN.

BY EDWARD WILLET.

I SAT at the edge of the battle,
  Though the shell around me burst;
And I watched the column charging,
  And felt that you were the first.

Through the smoke and the fire, the column
  Pressed onward again and again,
Till it melted under the tempest
  Of the terrible leaden rain.

Broken and shattered, the column
  Slowly drew out from the fight,
And my heart sank down within me,
  Sick at the sorrowful sight.

So few of that glorious column
  So sadly came back from the field:
Alas! they had fought too bravely;
  Oh! were it not better to yield?

But never the wife of a soldier
  Should grieve for the life she has given;
She gave it, — if God shall return it,
  So much she is owing to Heaven.

She gave it, — when battle shall claim it,
  Not hers, but her country 's the loss.
Ah ! well, she may weep for her country,
  And silently bear her cross.

I hoped, of the shells that were flying
  And bursting around me in air,
Some merciful one would strike me,
  At the edge of the battle there.

But back to the shattered column
  In safety I picked my way, —
Such pitying looks they gave me,
  But none had a word to say.

They led up your horse ; he was bloody,
  With the blood of the noble and true :
From his reeking side I kissed it,—
  It was all that was left me of you.

Oh, never the wife of a soldier
  Should grieve for the life she has given !
She gave it —if battle shall claim it,
  So much she has laid up in Heaven.

But the bullet that slew my darling
  Is piercing my poor heart through.

What tears I must shed for my country,
Though none I may weep for you!

THE SOLDIER'S LETTER.

HOW sweet, when night her misty veil
Around the weary soldier throws,
And twilight's golden skies grow pale,
And wooing winds invite repose,
To sit beside the watchfire's blaze,
Where friendly comrades nightly come,
To sing the song of other days,
And talk of things we love at home, —

Of those we love and list and wait,
Beneath the same benignant moon.
The postman's step behind the gate,
With tidings from the absent one;
And beaming smiles their thoughts reveal,
And love is mirrored in their eyes,
As eagerly they break the seal,
Elate with joy and glad surprise.

But dearer yet the shout that rings
In exultation loud and clear,

To hail the messenger who brings
  Letters from home and kindred dear;
And 'neath the pale moon's smiling light
  The soldier reads his treasure o'er;
And through the hours of silent night,
  In dreams he visits home once more.

In dreams he sits beside the hearth,
  Afar from camps and traitor's wiles,
And deems the dearest spot on earth
  Where loving wife and mother smiles;
And many a face almost forgot,
  And many a word so fondly spoken,
Come flitting round the soldier's cot,
  Till the sweet dream, at morn, is broken.

O ye who love the soldier well,
  Bid him be hopeful, brave, and gay;
Better he knows than you can tell,
  The perils that attend his way.
Some word of hope in battle's hour,
  While striving with a vengeful foe,
Has nerved the soldier's arm with power,
  To strike or ward the impending blow.

The soldier brave is often prone
  To deem himself forgotten quite,

A wanderer on the earth alone,
  When friends at home neglect to write.
Then cheer him oft with words like these,
  And thus your deep affection prove;
Let every keel that ploughs the seas
  Bear him some message full of love.

GOD SAVE THE NATION!

A WAR HYMN.*

BY THEODORE TILTON.

THOU who ordainest, for the land's salvation,
  Famine, and fire, and sword, and lamentation,
Now unto Thee we lift our supplication —
        God save the Nation!

By the great sign, foretold, of Thy Appearing,
Coming in clouds, while mortal men stand fearing,
Show us, amid this smoke of battle, clearing,
        Thy chariot nearing!

By the brave blood that floweth like a river,
Hurl Thou a thunderbolt from out Thy quiver!

* This hymn has been twelve times set to music.

Break Thou the strong gates! Every fetter shiver!
Smite and deliver!

Slay Thou our foes, or turn them to derision! —
Then, in the blood-red Valley of Decision,
Make the land green with Peace, as in a vision
Of fields elysian!

THE MEN WHO FELL IN BALTIMORE.

BY JOHN W. FORNEY.

OUR country's call awoke the land,
From mountain height to ocean strand;
The Old Keystone, the Bay State, too,
In all her direst dangers true,
Resolved to answer to her cry,
For her to bleed, for her to die;
And so they marched, their flag before,
For Washington, through Baltimore.

Our men from Berks and Schuylkill came —
Lehigh and Mifflin in their train:
First in the field, they sought the way,
Hearts beating high and spirits gay:
Heard the wild yells of fiendish spite,

Of armed mobs on left and right;
But on they marched, their flag before,
For Washington, through Baltimore.

Next came the Massachusetts men,
Gathered from city, glade, and glen:
No hate for South, but love for all,
They answered to their country's call.
The path to them seemed broad and bright;
They sought no foeman and no fight;
As on they marched, their flag before,
New England's braves, through Baltimore.

But when they showed their martial pride,
And closed their glittering columns wide,
They found their welcome in the fire
Of maddened foes and demons dire,
Who, like the fiends of hell sent forth,
Attacked these heroes of the North:
These heroes bold, with travel sore,
While on their way through Baltimore.

From every stifling den and street,
They rushed the gallant band to meet, —
Forgot the cause they came to save, —
Forgot that those they struck were brave, —
Forgot the dearest ties of blood

That bound them in one brotherhood, —
Forgot the flag that floated o'er
Their countrymen in Baltimore.

And the great song their son had penned,
To rally freemen to defend
The banner of the Stripes and Stars,
That makes victorious all our wars,
Was laughed to scorn, as madly then
They greeted all the gallant men
Who came from Massachusetts shore
To Washington, through Baltimore.

And when, with wildest grief, at last,
They saw their comrades falling fast,
Full on the hell-hounds in their track,
They wheeled, and drove the cowards back.
Then, with their hearts o'erwhelmed with woe,
Measured their progress, stern and slow;
Their wounded on their shoulders bore
To Washington, through Baltimore.

Yet, while New England mourns her dead,
The blood by Treason foully shed, —
Like that which flowed at Lexington,
When Freedom's earliest fight begun, —
Will make the day, the month, the year,

To every patriot's memory dear.
Sons of great fathers gone before,
They fell for Right at Baltimore!

As over every honored grave,
Where sleeps the "unreturning brave,"
A mother sobs, a young wife moans,
A father for his lost one groans,
Oh! let the people ne'er forget
Our deep, enduring, lasting debt
To those who left their native shore
And died for us in Baltimore.

THE PICKET-GUARD.

BY E. H.*

A LONELY spot! Dark forests dense,
For weary miles outstretch around,

* Very much of the soldier's picket duty in Western Virginia is performed in great, gloomy forests, with which the mountainous regions thereabouts are mainly covered. The picket post is usually on some obscure bridle-path away up in the mountain's side, or in the narrow ravine at its base, which divides it from its neighbor hills, all equally elevated, precipitous, and gloomy — and oftentimes miles distant from camp. The writer has him-

And far the lonely path from hence
  That echoes back the wagon's sound.

How monarch-like, leaf-crowned their forms,
  Uplift those noble pine and oak —
They know a hundred winter's storms,
  But not the axeman's ringing stroke.

A dreary night, nor moon nor star,
  Scarce yield one ray to cheer the gloom;
Away from camp and comrade far
  The picket, where may be his tomb.

The boughs o'erhead low bending grow,
  The moss beneath is old and green;
Amid the bushes crouching low,
  He peers, death-still, from forth between.

His rifle rests upon his knee,
  And on the stock two firm hands press;
Ah! well he knows how cheerily
  It heeds his fingers' quick caress.

self thus been picketed, where for days together not a soul was to be seen except the members of his own party. In such solitudes, the hush of night is sometimes broken by the bark of the wolf or the panther's plaintive cry, while the mountain fox frequently approaches almost within bayonet-thrust of the startled picket.

Three weary hours — or more — are gone;
The midnight must be drawing nigh;
The brooklet at his feet runs on,
He hears its murmuring melody.

A soothing sound! He thinks of home,
Of loved ones left at duty's call;
And flocking round him there they come,
The same old faces, forms, and all.

The gray-haired sire leans on his staff,
The matron lives with God in heaven;
He hears his brother's ringing laugh,
His sister's loving counsel given.

But there is yet another still,
A girlish form of simple grace;
How beats his heart, his pulses thrill,
Still gazing on that trusting face!

Not long! a near, quick, startling crash,
And home and friends and all are lost,
As where he looked for foeman's flash,
The prowling beast steals past his post.

The night wears on — a full hour more
Creeps drearily and slow away;

The moments pass the midnight hour,
  And glide into another day.

The winds arise; he hears o'erhead
  Their wrestlings in the upper deep;
He knows to-night the Storm-King dread
  No common revelry will keep.

Long-echoed through those forest aisles,
  The snuffing wolf his warning brays;
The answering cry from distant hills,
  The stealthy panther's haunt betrays.

The flitting nightbird's shrilly scream,
  Defiant of the gathering blast;
With hollow roar and fitful gleam,
  The storm around him bursts at last.

A fearful storm! The night is black,
  The torrent pours, the tree-tops reel,
And as it were dark doomsday's wreck,
  Red lightnings flash and thunders peal.

Against his sturdy tree close pressed,
  The picket's dripping form is leant,
And though no shelter, it is rest;
  Thank Heaven! the tempest's wrath is spent.

The quivering leaves their showers distil,
  The swollen stream sweeps madly on,
The north wind low is numbing chill
  To him that weary waits the dawn.

It comes at last — O beam of hope!
  Thank God that doth the day restore;
The sun mounts up the eastern slope,
  And, comrades, camp is gained once more.

Camp Elkwater, Va., Oct. 14, 1861.

WAR SONG.

DEDICATED TO THE MASSACHUSETTS REGIMENTS.

BY W. W. STORY.

UP with the Flag of the Stripes and the Stars!
  Gather together from plough and from loom!
Hark to the signal! — the music of wars
Sounding for tyrants and traitors their doom.
    March, march, march, march!
  Brothers unite — rouse in your might,
  For Justice and Freedom, for God and the Right!

Down with the foe to the Land and the Laws!
Marching together, our country to save,

God shall be with us to strengthen our cause,
Nerving the heart and the hand of the brave.
March, march, march, march!
Brothers unite — rouse in your might,
For Justice and Freedom, for God and the
Right!

Flag of the Free! under thee we will fight,
Shoulder to shoulder, our face to the foe;
Death to all traitors, and God for the Right!
Singing this song as to battle we go:
March, march, march, march!
Freemen unite — rouse in your might,
For Justice and Freedom, for God and the
Right!

Land of the Free — that our fathers of old,
Bleeding together, cemented in blood —
Give us thy blessing, as brave and as bold,
Standing like one, as our ancestors stood —
We march, march, march, march!
Conquer or fall! Hark to the call:
Justice and Freedom for one and for all!

Chain of the slave we have suffered so long —
Striving together, thy links we will break!
Hark! for God hears us, as echoes our song,

Sounding the cry to make Tyranny quake:
March, march, march, march! .
Conquer or fall! Rouse to the call —
Justice and Freedom for one and for all!

Workmen arise! There is work for us now;
Ours the red ledger for bayonet pen;
Sword be our hammer, and cannon our plough;
Liberty's loom must be driven by men!
March, march, march, march!
Freemen! we fight, roused in our might,
For Justice and Freedom, for God and the Right!

ELLSWORTH.

WHO is this ye say is slain?
Whose voice answers not again?
Ellsworth, shall we call in vain
On thy name to-day?
No! from every vale and hill
Our response all hearts shall thrill,
"Ellsworth's fame is with us still,
Ne'er to pass away!"

Bring that rebel banner low,
Hoisted by a treacherous foe:
'T was for that they dealt the blow,
Laid him in the dust.
Raise aloft, that all may see,
His loved flag of Liberty.
Forward, then, to victory,
Or perish if we must!

Hark to what Columbia saith:
"Mourn not for his early death,
With each patriot's dying breath
Strength renewed is given
To the cause of truth and right,
To the land for which they fight.
After darkness cometh light, —
Such the law of Heaven."

So we name him not in vain,
Though he comes not back again!
For his country he was slain;
Ellsworth's blood shall rise
To our gracious Saviour — King:
'T is a holy gift we bring;
Such a sacred offering
God will not despise.

FREEDOM.

BY MARTIN FARQUHAR TUPPER.

NO blots on the banner of Light!
No Slaves in the land of the Free!
No Wrong to be rampant where all should be Right,
No sin that is shameful to see!
America, — show the wide world in thy strength
How sternly determined thou art
To cut from thy soil, in its breadth and its length,
The canker that gnaws at thy heart!

Uprouse thee! and swear by thy Might
This evil no longer shall be;
For all men are brothers, the black as the white,
And sons of one Father are we!
America, — now is the perilous time,
When safety is solely decreed
To ridding the heart of old habits of crime,
And simply repenting indeed.

Away to the bats and the moles
With the lash and the goad and the chain!
Away with the buying and selling of souls,
And slavery toiling in pain!

America, this is thy chance — now at length —
  Of crushing — while crouching to thee —
Those Rebels and Slaveholders — slaves to thy
    strength, —
  The curse and contempt of the Free!

THE VOLUNTEER.

HARD by the porch of the village church,
  A dusty traveller halts awhile to rest;
  His head droops tired down upon his breast,
But the word of prayer wakes new life there.

" God bless the brave, who go to save
  Our country, in her dark, dread hour of danger!"
  The good man's voice was comfort to the stranger.
Duty wipes away a tear as he hurries to the war.

WAR SONG.

DEDICATED TO THE KENTUCKY STATE GUARD.

CHEER, boys, cheer, we 'll march away to battle,
  Cheer, boys, cheer, for our sweethearts and
    our wives;

Cheer, boys, cheer, we'll nobly do our duty,
And give to Kentucky our hearts, our arms, our lives.

Bring forth the flag, Kentucky's noble standard;
Wave it on high till the winds shake each fold out;
Proudly it floats, nobly waving in the vanguard:
Then cheer, boys, cheer, with a lusty, long, bold shout.
Cheer, boys, cheer, etc.

But though we march with heads all lowly bending,
Let us implore a blessing from on high;
Our cause is just, the Right from Wrong defending,
And the God of battles will listen to our cry.
Cheer, boys, cheer, etc.

Though to our homes we never may return,
Ne'er press again our loved ones in our arms,
O er our lone graves their faithful hearts will mourn:
Then cheer up, boys, cheer, such death hath no alarms.
Cheer, boys, cheer, etc.

BETHEL.

BY A. J. H. DUGANNE.

WE mustered at midnight, in darkness we formed,
And the whisper went round of a fort to be stormed;
But no drum-beat had called us, no trumpet we heard,
And no voice of command, but our Colonel's low word, —
"Column! Forward!"

And out, through the mist and the murk of the morn,
From the beaches of Hampton our barges were borne;
And we heard not a sound, save the sweep of the oar,
Till the word of our Colonel came up from the shore, —
"Column! Forward!"

With hearts bounding bravely, and eyes all alight,
As ye dance to soft music, so trod we that night;

Through the aisles of the greenwood, with vines
overarched,
Tossing dew-drops, like gems, from our feet, as we
marched, —
"Column! Forward!"

As ye dance with the damsels, to viol and flute,
So we skipped from the shadows, and mocked their
pursuit;
But the soft zephyrs chased us, with scents of the
morn,
As we passed by the hay-fields and green waving
corn, —
"Column! Forward!"

For the leaves were all laden with fragrance of
June,
And the flowers and the foliage with sweets were
in tune;
And the air was so calm, and the forest so dumb,
That we heard our own heart-beats, like taps of a
drum, —
"Column! Forward!"

Till the lull of the lowlands was stirred by a breeze,
And the buskins of Morn brushed the tops of the
trees,

And the glintings of glory that slid from her track
By the sheen of our rifles were gayly flung back,—
"Column! Forward!"

And the woodlands grew purple with sunshiny mist,
And the blue-crested hill-tops with rose-light were kissed,
And the earth gave her prayers to the sun in perfumes,
Till we marched as through gardens, and trampled on blooms,—
"Column! Forward!"

Ay! trampled on blossoms, and seared the sweet breath
Of the green-wood with low-brooding vapors of death;
O'er the flowers and the corn we were borne like a blast,
And away to the forefront of battle we passed,—
"Column! Forward!"

For the cannon's hoarse thunder roared out from the glades,
And the sun was like lightning on banners and blades,

When the long line of chanting Zouaves, like a
flood,
From the green of the woodlands rolled, crimson as
blood, —
"Column! Forward!"

While the sound of their song, like the surge of the
seas,
With the "Star-Spangled Banner" swelled over
the leas;
And the sword of Duryea, like a torch, led the
way,
Bearing down on the batteries of Bethel that
day, —*
"Column! Forward!"

Through green-tasselled cornfields our columns
were thrown,
And like corn by the red scythe of fire we were
mown;

* The march on Bethel was begun in high spirits, at midnight, but it was near noon when the Zouaves, in their crimson uniform, led by Colonel Duryea, charged the batteries, after singing the "Star-Spangled Banner" in chorus. Major Winthrop fell in the storming of the enemy's defences, and was left on the battle-field. Lieut. Greble, the only other officer killed, was shot at his gun soon after. This fatal contest inaugurated the "war of posts" which raged in Virginia.

While the cannon's fierce ploughings new-furrowed
the plain,
That our blood might be planted for LIBERTY'S
grain, —
"Column! Forward!"

Oh! the fields of fair June have no lack of sweet
flowers,
But their rarest and best breathe no fragrance like
ours;
And the sunshine of June, sprinkling gold on the
corn,
Hath no harvest that ripeneth like BETHEL'S red
morn, —
"Column! Forward!"

When our heroes, like bridegrooms, with lips and
with breath,
Drank the first kiss of Danger and clasped her in
death;
And the heart of brave WINTHROP grew mute,
with his lyre,
When the plumes of his genius lay moulting in
fire, —
"Column! Forward!"

Where he fell shall be sunshine as bright as his
name,

And the grass where he slept shall be green as his
fame;
For the gold of the Pen and the steel of the
Sword
Write his deeds — in his blood — on the land he
adored, —
"Column! Forward!"

And the soul of our comrade shall sweeten the
air,
And the flowers and the grass-blades his memory
upbear;
While the breath of his genius, like music in leaves,
With the corn-tassels whispers, and sings in the
sheaves, —
"Column! Forward!"

NORTHMEN, COME OUT!

DEDICATED TO THE MASSACHUSETTS REGIMENTS.

BY CHARLES GODFREY LELAND.

(AIR — *Burschen heraus!*)

NORTHMEN, come out!
Forth unto battle with storm and shout!
Freedom calls you once again,

To flag and fort and tented plain;
Then come with drum and trump and song,
And raise the war-cry wild and strong:
Northmen, come out!

Northmen, come out!
The foe is waiting round about,
With paixhan, mortar, and petard,
To tender us their Beau-regard;
With shot and shrapnell, grape and shell,
We 'll give them back the fire of hell:
Northmen, come out!

Northmen, come out!
Give the pirates a roaring rout;
Out in your strength and let them know
How Working Men to Work can go.
Out in your might and let them feel
How Mudsills strike when edged with steel:
Northmen, come out!

Northmen, come out!
Come like your grandsires stern and stout;
Though Cotton be of Kingly stock,
Yet royal heads may reach the block;
The Puritan taught it once in pain,
His sons shall teach it once again:
Northmen, come out!

Northmen, come out!
Forth into battle with storm and shout!
He who lives with victory's blest,
He who dies gains peaceful rest.
Living or dying, let us be
Still vowed to God and Liberty!
Northmen, come out!

PRO PATRIA.

INSCRIBED TO THE SECOND NEW HAMPSHIRE REGIMENT.

BY THOMAS BAILEY ALDRICH.

I.

THE grand old earth shakes at the tread of the Norsemen,
Who meet, as of old, in defence of the true;
All hail to the stars that are set in their banner!
All hail to the red, and the white, and the blue!
As each column wheels by,
Hear their hearts' battle-cry,—
It was Warren's,—*'Tis sweet for our country to die!*

II.

Lancaster and Coos, Laconia and Concord,
Old Portsmouth and Keene, send their stalwart young men;

They come from the plough, and the loom, and the
anvil,
From the marge of the sea, from the hill-top and
glen.
As each column wheels by,
Hear their hearts' battle-cry,—
It was Warren's,—*'Tis sweet for our country to die!*

III.

The prayers of fair women, like legions of angels,
Watch over our soldiers by day and by night;
And the King of all glory, the Chief of all armies,
Shall love them and lead them who dare to be
right!
As each column wheels by,
Hear their hearts' battle-cry,—
It was Warren's,—*'Tis sweet for our country to die!*

THE PICKET-GUARD.

"ALL quiet along the Potomac," they say,
"Except now and then a stray picket
Is shot, as he walks on his beat, to and fro,
By a rifleman hid in the thicket.

'T is nothing — a private or two, now and then,
  Will not count in the news of the battle;
Not an officer lost — only one of the men,
  Moaning out, all alone, the death-rattle."

All quiet along the Potomac to-night,
  Where the soldiers lie peacefully dreaming;
Their tents, in the rays of the clear autumn moon,
  Or the light of the watch-fires are gleaming.
A tremulous sigh, as the gentle night-wind
  Through the forest leaves softly is creeping;
While stars up above, with their glittering eyes,
  Keep guard — for the army is sleeping.

There 's only the sound of the lone sentry's tread
  As he tramps from the rock to the fountain,
And thinks of the two in the low trundle-bed,
  Far away in the cot on the mountain.
His musket falls slack, — his face, dark and grim,
  Grows gentle with memories tender,
As he mutters a prayer for the children asleep, —
  For their mother, — may Heaven defend her!

The moon seems to shine just as brightly as then,
  That night, when the love yet unspoken
Leaped up to his lips, — when low, murmured vows
  Were pledged to be ever unbroken.

Then drawing his sleeve roughly over his eyes,
  He dashes off tears that are welling,
And gathers his gun closer up to its place,
  As if to keep down the heart-swelling.

He passes the fountain, the blasted pine-tree —
  The footstep is lagging and weary;
Yet onward he goes, through the broad belt of light,
  Toward the shades of the forest so dreary.
Hark! was it the night-wind that rustled the leaves?
  Was it moonlight so wondrously flashing?
It looked like a rifle — "Ha! MARY, good-by!"
  And the life-blood is ebbing and plashing.

All quiet along the Potomac to-night, —
  No sound save the rush of the river;
While soft falls the dew on the face of the dead, —
  The picket 's off duty forever.

THE HOLY WAR.

BY MRS. HARRIET BEECHER STOWE.

"And I saw heaven opened, and beheld a white horse; and He that sat upon him was called Faithful and True, and in righteousness He doth judge and make war. His eyes were as a flame of fire, and on His head were many crowns; and He had a name written, that no man knew, but He himself. And the armies which were in heaven followed Him upon white horses, clothed in fine linen, white and clean." — *Rev.* xix. 11, 12, 14.

TO the last battle set, throughout the earth!
Not for vile lust of plunder or of power,
The hosts of justice and eternal right
Unfurl their banner in this solemn hour.

A King rides forth, whose eyes, as burning fire,
Wither oppression in their dazzling flame;
And He hath sworn to right all human wrong,
By the dread power of His mysterious name.

O'er all the earth resounds His trumpet-call.
The nations, waking from their dreary night,
Are mustering in their ranks, and thronging on
To hail the brightness of His rising light:

And all the armies that behind Him ride,
Come in white raiment, spotless as the snow;

"Freedom and Justice" is their battle-cry,
  And all the earth rejoices as they go.

Shoulder to shoulder ride the brother bands, —
  Brave hearts and tender, with undaunted eye;
With manly patience ready to endure,
  With gallant daring resolute to die.

They know not fear, for what have they to fear
  Who *all* have counted, and have *all* resigned,
And laid their lives a solemn offering down
  For laws, for truth, for freedom, — for mankind?

No boastful words are theirs, nor murderous zeal,
  Nor courage fed with the inebriate bowl;
But their brave hearts show in true touch and time
  The sober courage of the manly soul.

Ah! who can say how precious and how dear
  Those noble hearts, of thousand homes the light?
Yet wives and mothers, smiling through their tears,
  Gave them, unmurmuring, to the holy fight.

O brothers, banded for this sacred war!
  Keep your white garments spotless still and pure;
Be priestly warriors, hallowing the right, —
  So shall your victory be swift and sure.

So shall the spotless King with whom ye ride
  Make vile disorder from the earth to cease;
And Time's triumphant songs at last shall hail
  The victory of a true and righteous peace.

JULY 21ST, 1861.

BY A. L.

THE dawn in Virginia came forth in its beauty,
  The stars glimmered softly, then faded away;
And many a soldier rose up to his duty,
To fight for the Union and Freedom that day.

The morning wind stirs — like some far-off loved fingers —
The plumes of the chieftains with flickering breath;
And Victory follows, and hovers, and lingers, —
Alas, but o'er those that are marching to death!

How fairly the columns step out in their order,
Their bayonets gleam in the dim dusky light;
Their music plays "Dixie," and "Over the Border,"
Down the long dusty road as they march to the fight.

How soft on yon hill-side the young trees are wav-
ing, —
How peaceful the fields lie in summer's display ;
O soldiers ! you know not the perils you 're brav-
ing !
O leaders, be wary ! look well to the way !

Those iron-wrought guns that lie hid in the distance,
Those batteries planted to check our hot haste, —
More tender their mercies, more kind their resist-
ance,
Than that of the Rebels by whom they are placed !

Brave enemies they ; though stern-hearted you 'll
find them,
Their open-mouthed vengeance is honestly sped ;
But cowards and savages lurk there behind them,
Who sabre the dying and mangle the dead.

Alas for the South ! — was her fame all unfounded ?
Her praises are royal, — believe them who list ;
But her brave soldiers aim at the fallen and wounded,
And the "chivalry" strike — those who cannot re-
sist !

Let History tell — for her words will not quiver,
Her eyes will see clearly, her heart will be still —

The tale of that once all unknown little river
That flows at the base of Manassas Gap Hill.

Let History tell with what brave, eager daring
Our troops faced the cannon that day at Bull Run;
The fierce iron hail, like a winter storm bearing,
Till the battle was lost which their blood had just won.

Let her say they retreated; — then add, they were fainting
With hunger and thirst and the strife of a day;
And point to the number dropped down in deep slumber,
On their arms and the greensward to rest by the way!

How silent, how dreamless a sleep hath descended
On yonder red field where their friends are at rest!
Unguarded they lie, — undisturbed, undefended, —
Only Honor keeps watch by each low-lying crest.

The fitful night-wind sighs its wild lamentation,
The soft-falling dew drops cold tears on their bed;
But heavy and hot will the tears of the Nation
Pour down at the feet of her Volunteer dead!

Tramp, tramp, through the darkness, with "Steady! men, steady!"
In stillness and sadness the columns pass by;
Driven back from the trenches, in which they were ready
To give their young life-blood, and conquer or die.

O morning! O daylight! in glory awaking,
How can ye come forth after such a black night?
And with the full burst of the sunbeams outbreaking
Look down on the tokens of death and of flight!

The morning turned gray: and then thicker and faster
The rain with its driving mist sullenly came:
It could not wash off the dark signs of disaster,
Nor tarnish the glory, nor blot out the shame.

TO THE MEN OF THE NORTH AND WEST.

BY R. H. STODDARD.

MEN of the North and West,
Wake in your might,
Prepare, as the Rebels have done,
For the fight!

You cannot shrink from the test,
Rise! Men of the North and West!

They have torn down your banner of stars;
They have trampled the laws;
They have stifled the freedom they hate,
For no cause!
Do you love it or slavery best?
Speak! Men of the North and West.

They strike at the life of the State: —
Shall the murder be done?
They cry, "We are two!" And you?
"*We are one!*"
You must meet them, then, breast to breast;
On! Men of the North and West!

Not with words; they laugh them to scorn,
And tears they despise;
But with swords in your hands, and death
In your eyes!
Strike home! leave to God all the rest,
Strike! Men of the North and West!

HARVARD STUDENT'S SONG.

BY JULIA WARD HOWE.

(*Denkst du daran.*)

REMEMBER ye the fateful gun that sounded
To Sumter's walls from Charleston's treacherous shore?
Remember ye how hearts indignant bounded
When our first dead came back from Baltimore?
The banner fell that every breeze had flattered,
The hum of thrift was hushed with sudden woe;
We raised anew the emblems shamed and shattered,
And turned a front resolved to meet the foe.

Remember ye, how forth to battle faring
Our valiant ranks the fierce attack withstood,
In all the terrors of the tumult bearing
The people's heart of dauntless lionhood?
How many a hand forsook its wonted labor,
Forsook its gains, as prizes fall'n in worth,
To wield with pain the warlike lance and sabre,
To conquer Peace with God, for all on earth?

Remember ye, how, out of boyhood leaping,
Our gallant mates stood ready for the fray;

As new-fledged eaglets rise, with sudden sweeping,
And meet unscared the dazzling front of day ?
Our classic toil became inglorious leisure,
We praised the calm Horatian ode no more ;
But answered back with song the martial measure,
That held its throb above the cannon's roar.

Remember ye the pageants dim and solemn,
Where Love and Grief have borne the funeral pall ?
The joyless marching of the mustered column,
With arms reversed to Him who conquers all ?
Oh ! give them back, thou bloody breast of Treason,
They were our own, the darlings of our hearts !
They come benumbed and frosted out of season,
With whom the summer of our youth departs.

Look back no more ! our time has come, my Brothers !
In Fate's high roll our names are written too ;
We fill the mournful gaps left bare by others,
The ranks where Fear has never broken through !
Look, ancient walls, upon our stern election !
Keep, Echoes dear, remembrance of our breath !
And, gentle eyes and hearts of pure affection,
Light us, resolved to Victory or Death !

KISS ME, MOTHER, AND LET ME GO.

BY MISS NANCY A. W. PRIEST.

HAVE you heard the news that I heard to-day?
  The news that trembles on every lip?
The sky is darker again, they say,
  And breakers threaten the good old ship.
Our country calls on her sons again,
  To strike, in her name, at a dastard foe;
She asks for six hundred thousand men;
  I would be one, mother. Let me go.

The love of country was born with me;
  I remember how my young heart would thrill
When I used to sit on my grandame's knee
  And list to the story of Bunker Hill.
Life gushed out there in a rich red flood;
  My grandsire fell in that fight, you know;—
Would you have me shame the brave old blood?
  Nay, kiss me, mother, and let me go.

Our flag, the flag of our hope and pride,
  With its stars and stripes, and its field of blue,
Is mocked, insulted, torn down, defied,
  And trampled upon by the rebel crew.
And England and France look on and sneer,

"Ha! queen of the earth, thou art fallen low;"
Earth's downtrod millions weep and fear;
So kiss me, mother, and let me go.

Under the burning Southern skies,
Our brothers languish in heart-sick pain,
They turn to us with their pleading eyes;
O mother, say, shall they turn in vain?
Their ranks are thinning from sun to sun,
Yet bravely they hold at bay the foe;
Shall we let them die there, one by one?
So kiss me, mother, and let me go.

Can you selfishly cling to your household joys,
Refusing this smallest tithe to yield,
While thousands of mothers are sending boys
Beloved as yours to the battle-field?
Can you see my country call in vain,
And restrain my arm from the needful blow?
Not so, though your heart should break with pain,
You will kiss me, mother, and let me go.

A MOTHER'S ANSWER.

"I HAVE KISSED HIM, AND LET HIM GO."

HE'S my own boy, and this is my plea:
 Perhaps it is foolish and weak;
But mothers I'm sure will have pity on me,
 And some word will tenderly speak.
The light of my home — my tears fall like rain —
 Is it wonder I shrink from the blow —
That my heart is crushed by its weight of pain?
 But I've kissed him, and let him go.

There are some, I know, who feel a strange pride
 In giving their country their all, —
Who count it a glory that boys from their side,
 In the strife are ready to fall.
But I, sitting here, have no pride in my heart;
 (God forgive me that this should be so!)
For the boy that I love the tears still start,
 Yet I've kissed him, and let him go.

Last night, with soft steps, I stole to his bed
 As oft in childhood I'd done;
On his pillow I bowed my poor, stricken head
 Till out of the east rose the sun.
His dreams were of me; for he turned in his sleep,

And murmured "Dear mother!" so low,
I bit my pale lips lest they 'd cowardly speak
"O, my darling, *I can't let you go!*"

This morning I blessed him; I stifled my pain;
I bade him be true to his trust;
To stand by the flag till his country again
Should raise its proud head from the dust.
I knew by the light in his beautiful eyes, —
By his face with true courage aglow, —
He 'd fight to the last. I choked back my sighs,
While I kissed him, and let him go.

But oh, sitting here, this desolate day,
Still there comes no feeling of pride;
But One knows my need, and to Him will I pray,
I can trust Him whatever betide.
And if he shall fall, — (O, faint heart, be still!)
I know He will soften the blow,
And I yet may feel a patriot's thrill
That I kissed him, and let him go.

THE BATTLE SUMMER.

BY HENRY T. TUCKERMAN.

THE summer wanes, — her languid sighs now yield
To autumn's cheering air;
The teeming orchard and the waving field
Fruition's glory wear.

More clear against the flushed horizon wall,
Stand forth each rock and tree;
More near the cricket's note, the plover's call,
More crystalline the sea.

The sunshine chastened, like a mother's gaze,
The meadow's vagrant balm;
The purple leaf and amber-tinted maize
Reprove us while they calm;

For on the landscape's brightly pensive face,
War's angry shadows lie;
His ruddy stains upon the woods we trace,
And in the crimson sky.

No more we bask in Earth's contented smile,
But sternly muse apart;

Vainly her charms the patriot's soul beguile,
Or woo the orphan's heart.

Yon keen-eyed stars with mute reproaches brand
The lapse from faith and law, —
No more harmonious emblems of a land
Ensphered in love and awe.

As cradled in the noontide's warm embrace,
And bathed in dew and rain,
The herbage freshened, and in billowy grace
Wide surged the ripening grain;

And the wild rose and clover's honeyed cell
Exhaled their peaceful breath,
On the soft air broke Treason's fiendish yell, —
The harbinger of death!

Nor to the camp alone his summons came,
To blast the glowing day,
But heavenward bore upon the wings of flame
Our poet's mate away; *

And set his seal upon the statesman's lips
On which a nation hung; †
And rapt the noblest life in cold eclipse,
By woman lived or sung. ‡

* Mrs. Longfellow. † Cavour. ‡ Mrs. Browning.

How shrinks the heart from Nature's festal noon,
As shrink the withered leaves, —
In the wan-light of Sorrow's harvest-moon
To glean her blighted sheaves.

Newport, R. I., September, 1861.

A RAINY DAY IN CAMP.

BY MRS. ROBERT SHAW HOWLAND.

IT 'S a cheerless, lonesome evening,
When the soaking, sodden ground
Will not echo to the footfall
Of the sentinel's dull round.

God's blue star-spangled banner
To-night is not unfurled,
Surely *He* has not deserted
This weary, warring world.

I peer into the darkness,
And the crowding fancies come;
The night-wind, blowing Northward
Carries all my heart toward home.

For I 'listed in this army
Not exactly to my mind;

But my country called for helpers,
  And I could n't stay behind.

So, I 've had a sight of drilling,
  And have roughed it many ways,
And Death has nearly had me ;
  Yet I think the service pays.

It 's a blessed sort of feeling,
  Whether you live or die ;
You helped your country in her need,
  And fought right loyally.

But I can't help thinking, sometimes,
  When a wet day's leisure comes,
That I hear the old home voices
  Talking louder than the drums,

And the far, familiar faces
  Peep in at the tent door,
And the little children's footsteps
  Go pit-pat on the floor,

I can't help thinking, somehow,
  Of all the parson reads
About that other Soldier-life
  Which every true man leads.

And wife, soft-hearted creature,
  Seems a-saying in my ear,
"I'd rather have you in *those* ranks
  Than to see you Brigadier."

I call myself a brave one,
  But in my héart I lie!
For my Country and her Honor
  I am fiercely free to die.

But when the Lord who bought me,
  Asks for my service here,
To "fight the good fight" faithfully,
  I'm skulking in the rear.

And yet I know this Captain
  All love and care to be;
He would never get impatient
  With a raw recruit like me.

And I know He'd not forget me,
  When the Day of Peace appears;
I should share with Him the victory
  Of all his volunteers.

And it's kind of cheerful, thinking
  Beside the dull tent fire,

About that big promotion
  When He says, " Come up higher."

And though it 's dismal rainy,
  Even now, with thoughts of Him,
Camp-life looks extra cheery,
  And death a deal less grim.

For I seem to see Him waiting
  Where a gathered Heaven greets
A great, victorious army,
  Surging up the golden streets ;

And I hear Him read the roll-call,
  And my heart is all aflame,
When the dear, Recording Angel
  Writes down my happy name !

But my fire is dead white ashes,
  And the tent is chilling cold,
And I 'm playing *win the battle*,
  When I 've never been enrolled.

BY THE BANKS OF THE CUMBERLAND.

BY S. C. MERCER.

BY the banks of the Cumberland echoes the roar
Of the sentinel's warning, — the foe's on the shore!
Our war-drums are beaten, our bugles are blown,
And our legions advance to their musical tone.

By the banks of the Cumberland, slippery and red,
With the death-dew of battle, and strewn with the dead,
Kentucky has routed her insolent foe,
And victory's star gilds the night of our woe.

By those banks, that once bloomed like an Eden of joy,
The demon of treason stalked forth to destroy;
Our rich teeming harvests he swept in his wrath,
And the blaze of our dwellings illumined his path.

Like an eagle-plumed arrow our Nemesis comes,
Shout, soldiers! sound, bugles! and clamor, O drums!
Let the land ring aloud in the wildness of joy,
And the bonfires blaze brightly, — but not to destroy.

For the God of the Union has prospered the right,
And the cohorts of treason have melted in flight.
Blow, bugles! roll, river! and tell to the sea
That our swords shall not rest 'till Kentucky is
free.

THE FLOWER OF LIBERTY.

BY OLIVER WENDELL HOLMES.

WHAT flower is this that greets the morn,
Its hues from heaven so freshly born?
With burning star and flaming band
It kindles all the sunset land;—
O, tell us what its name may be!
Is this the Flower of Liberty?
It is the banner of the free,
The starry Flower of Liberty!

In savage Nature's far abode
Its tender seed our fathers sowed;
The storm-winds rocked its swelling bud,
Its opening leaves were streaked with blood,
Till, lo! earth's tyrants shook to see
The full-blown Flower of Liberty!
Then hail the banner of the free,
The starry Flower of Liberty!

Behold its streaming rays unite
One mingling flood of braided light, —
The red that fires the Southern rose,
With spotless white from Northern snows,
And, spangled o'er its azure, see
The sister Stars of Liberty!
    Then hail the banner of the free,
    The starry Flower of Liberty!

The blades of heroes fence it round;
Where'er it springs is holy ground;
From tower and dome its glories spread;
It waves where lonely sentries tread;
It makes the land as ocean free,
And plants an empire on the sea!
    Then hail the banner of the free,
    The starry Flower of Liberty!

Thy sacred leaves, fair Freedom's flower,
Shall ever float on dome and tower,
To all their heavenly colors true,
In blackening frost or crimson dew, —
And God love us as we love thee,
Thrice holy Flower of Liberty!
    Then hail the banner of the free,
    The starry Flower of Liberty!

"NEWS FROM THE WAR."

ANONYMOUS.

TWO women sit at a farm-house door,
  Busily reading the news,
While softly around them fair twilight sheds
  Her tender shadows and dews.

Peace smiles in the cloudless heaven above;
  Peace rests on the landscape fair;
And peace, like a holy spirit of love,
  Broods in the balmy air.

But not one ray of peace illumes
  Those sad and wistful eyes,
Which search that printed record o'er
  As mariners search the skies.

Look on their faces: one like a rose
  Fresh with the beauty of May;
The other, pale as a waning moon
  Seen through thin clouds of gray.

Yet, though one is young and the other old,
  With the same soft glory they shine;
For they 're tinted with tenderest light and shades
  By Love, the artist divine.

Now, fast as a radiant vision, fades
  The glow of the western skies;
Yet the readers read on, — unmindful of all
  Save the paper before their eyes.

Nothing to them the charms of that hour, —
  The magic of meadow and hill;
For spirits bowed down with a weight of care,
  Are blind to the beautiful still.

Deeper the shadows of twilight fall;
  More hushed grows the dewy air,
When suddenly breaks on that holy calm
  A quick, wild cry of despair.

The younger glances have found it first, —
  That record so sad and so brief;
"Mortally wounded!" — two dread words —
  Winged arrows of pain and grief.

"Mortally wounded!" — look again;
  Alas! it is all too true;
Not the brave alone, but the fond and fair
  Are mortally wounded, too.

He, on the battle-field far away;
  They, in their quiet home, —

The wife and the mother, who never more
 Shall see their loved hero come.

The grass will grow where the warrior fell,
 And sweet wild flowers may bloom
On the very turf once blackened and burned
 By the fearful fires of doom.

But the smiling summers, that come and go,
 Can never, never heal
The bleeding bosoms which felt to-day
 Something sharper than steel.

"Mortally wounded!" oh, dread War!
 Many a victim is thine,
Save those who hear your terrible voice
 Go thundering along the line!

If we give proud names and echoing hymns,
 And build up monuments grand
To the gallant spirits who suffer and fall
 In defence of their native land;

Let us yield a tenderer tribute still, —
 Sad tears and a pitying sigh, —
To the uncrowned martyrs who silently sink,
 And die when their heroes die.

MARCH!

BY BAYARD TAYLOR.

WITH rushing winds and gloomy skies
The dark and stubborn Winter dies;
Far-off, unseen, Spring faintly cries,
Bidding her earliest child arise:
March!

By streams still held in icy snare,
On Southern hill-sides, melting bare,
O'er fields that motley colors wear,
That summons fills the changeful air:
March!

What though conflicting seasons make
Thy days their field, they woo or shake
The sleeping lids of Life awake,
And Hope is stronger for thy sake:
March!

Then from thy mountains, ribbed with snow,
Once more thy rousing bugle blow,
And East and West, and to and fro,
Proclaim thy coming to the foe:
March!

Say to the picket, chilled and numb,
Say to the camp's impatient hum,
Say to the trumpet and the drum:
Lift up your hearts, I come, I come!
March!

Cry to the waiting hosts that stray
On sandy sea-sides far away,
By marshy isle and gleaming bay,
Where Southern March is Northern May:
March!

Announce thyself with welcome noise,
Where Glory's victor-eagles poise
Above the proud, heroic boys
Of Iowa and Illinois:
March!

Then down the long Potomac's line
Shout like a storm on hills of pine,
Till ramrods ring and bayonets shine, —
"Advance! the Chieftain's call is mine:
"MARCH!"

ACROSS THE LINES.

BY ETHEL LYNN.

LEFT for dead? I — Charlie Coleman,
  On the field we won — and lost,
Like a dog; the ditch my death-bed,
  My pillow but a log across.
Helpless hangs my arm beside me,
  Drooping lies my aching head;
How strange it sounded when that soldier,
  Passing, spoke of me as "dead."

Dead? and here — where yonder banner
  Flaunts its scanty group of stars,
And that rebel emblem binds me
  Close within those bloody bars.
Dead? without a stone to tell it,
  Nor a flower above my breast!
Dead? where none will whisper softly,
  "Here a brave man lies at rest!"

Help me, Thou, my mother's Helper, —
  Jesus, Thou who biding here,
Loved like me an earthly mother,
  Be thou still to aid me near.

Give me strength to totter yonder,
  Hold me up till o'er me shines
The flag of Union, — there she promised
  To meet me, just beyond the lines.

Well I know how she will wander
  Where a woman's foot may stray,
Looking with those eyes so tender
  Where the poor boys wounded lay.
How her hand will bring them water,
  For her own boy Charlie's sake,
And when dying bid them whisper,
  "I pray the Lord my soul to take."

Ah! I stand on foot but feebly,
  And the blood runs very fast,
Yet by fence and bush I'll stagger
  Till the rebel lines be passed.
"Courage, Charlie! twist it tighter, —
  The tourniquet about your arm;
Be a man — don't faint and shiver
  When the lifetide trickles warm."

Faint and weak, — still coming, mother,
  Walking some, but creeping more,
Fearing lest the watchful sentry
  Stops the heart-beat, — slow before.

Stay — with fingers ruddy dabbled
  Loose the belt your waist confines;
Write upon it " Charlie Coleman —
  Carry him across the lines."

Trembling letters, — but some stranger
  Chance may read them when I 'm gone,
And for the sake of love and pity
  Bear my lifeless body on.
Coming! ah — what means this darkness —
  Night too soon is coming on.
Mother, are you waiting? — " Jesus,
  Tell her that with You I 've gone."

Then the head her heart had pillowed,
  Drooping laid it down to rest,
As calm as when in baby slumber
  Its locks were cradled on her breast.

. . . .

Glowed the sunset o'er the meadow,
  Lighting up the gloomy pines,
Where a body only lingered —
  Charlie's soul had crossed the lines.

A passing soldier — foe, yet human —
  Stooped to read the words of blood;
So pitiful, so sadly earnest;
  And bore him onward through the wood.

Beneath the white flag bore him safely.
Now, while Indian Summer shines,
A mother's tears dew springing myrtle,
O'er Charlie's grave across the lines.

THE CAPTAIN'S WIFE.

BY THEODORE TILTON.

WE gathered roses, Blanche and I, for little Madge one morning;
"Like every soldier's wife," said Blanche, "I dread a soldier's fate."
Her voice a little trembled then, as under some forewarning.
A soldier galloped up the lane, and halted at the gate.

"Which house is Malcolm Blake's?" he cried; "a letter for his sister!"
And when I thanked him, Blanche inquired, "But none for me, his wife?"
The soldier played with Madge's curls, and, stooping over, kissed her:
"Your father was my captain, child!—I loved him as my life!"

Then suddenly he galloped off and left the rest
unspoken.
I burst the seal, and Blanche exclaimed, — " What
makes you tremble so ? "
What answer did I dare to speak ? How ought the
news be broken ?
I could not shield her from the stroke, yet tried to
ease the blow.

" A battle in the swamps," I said ; " our men were
brave, but lost it."
And, pausing there, — " The note," I said, " is not
in Malcolm's hand."
And first a flush flamed through her face, and then
a shadow crossed it.
" Read quick, dear May ! — read all, I pray — and
let me understand ! "

I did not read it as it stood, — but tempered so the
phrases
As not at first to hint the worst, — held back the
fatal word,
And half retold his gallant charge, his shout, his
comrades' praises —
Till like a statue carved in stone, she neither spoke
nor stirred !

Oh, never yet a woman's heart was frozen so completely!
So unbaptized with helping tears! — so passionless and dumb!
Spellbound she stood, and motionless, — till little Madge spoke sweetly:
"Dear mother, is the battle done? and will my father come?"

I laid my finger on her lips, and set the child to playing.
Poor Blanche! the winter in her cheek was snowy like her name!
What could she do but kneel and pray, — and linger at her praying?
O Christ! when other heroes die, moan other wives the same?

Must other women's hearts yet break, to keep the Cause from failing?
God pity our brave lovers then, who face the battle's blaze!
And pity wives in widowhood! — But is it unavailing?
O Lord! give Freedom first, then Peace! — and unto Thee be praise!

THE DEFENDERS.

BY THOMAS BUCHANAN READ.

OUR flag on the land and our flag on the ocean,
  An angel of peace wheresoever it goes;
Nobly sustained by Columbia's devotion,
  The angel of death it shall be to our foes!
    True to its native sky
    Still shall our eagle fly,
Casting his sentinel glances afar;
    Though bearing the olive branch,
    Still in his talons stanch
Grasping the bolts of the thunders of war!

Hark to the sound! There 's a foe on our border,—
  A foe striding on to the gulf of his doom;
Freemen are rising and marching in order,
  Leaving the plough and the anvil and loom.
    Rust dims the harvest sheen
    Of scythe and of sickle keen;
The axe sleeps in peace by the tree it would mar;
    Veteran and youth are out
    Swelling the battle shout,
Grasping the bolts of the thunders of war!

Our brave mountain eagles swoop from their eyry,
  Our little panthers leap from forest and plain

Out of the West flash the flames of the prairie, —
  Out of the East roll the waves of the main:
    Down from their northern shores,
    Swift as Niagara pours,
They march, and their tread wakes the earth with its jar;
    Under the Stripes and Stars,
    Each with the soul of Mars,
Grasping the bolts of the thunders of war!

Spite of the sword or assassin's stiletto,
  While throbs a heart in the breast of the brave,
The oak of the North or the Southern palmetto
  Shall shelter no foe except in the grave!
    While the gulf billow breaks
    Echoing the northern lakes,
And ocean replies unto ocean afar,
    Yield we no inch of land
    While there 's a patriot hand
Grasping the bolts of the thunders of war!

Rome, July 4, 1861.

CARTE DE VISITE.

ANONYMOUS.

'TWAS a terrible fight," the soldier said !
" Our Colonel was one of the first to fall,
Shot dead on the field by a rifle ball, —
A braver heart than his never bled."

A group for the painter's art were they :
The soldier with scarred and sunburnt face,
A fair-haired girl, full of youth and grace,
And her aged mother, wrinkled and gray.

These three in porch, where the sunlight came
Through the tangled leaves of the jasmine-vine,
Spilling itself like a golden wine,
And flecking the doorway with rings of flame.

The soldier had stopped to rest by the way,
For the air was sultry with summer-heat ;
The road was like ashes under the feet,
And a weary distance before him lay.

" Yes, a terrible fight : our Ensign was shot
As the order to charge was given the men,

When one from the ranks seized our colors, and then
He, too, fell dead on the self-same spot.

"A handsome boy was this last: his hair
Clustered in curls round his noble brow;
I can almost fancy I see him now,
With the scarlet stain on his face so fair."

"What was his name? — have you never heard? —
Where was he from, this youth who fell?
And your regiment, stranger, which was it? tell!"
"Our regiment? It was the Twenty-third."

The color fled from the young girl's cheek,
Leaving it as white as the face of the dead;
The mother lifted her eyes, and said:
"Pity my daughter — in mercy speak!"

"I never knew aught of this gallant youth,"
The soldier answered; not even his name,
Or from what part of our State he came: —
As God is above, I speak the truth!

"But when we buried our dead that night,
I took from his breast this picture, — see!
It is as like him as like can be:
Hold it this way, toward the light."

One glance, and a look, half-sad, half-wild,
  Passed over her face, which grew more pale,
  Then a passionate, hopeless, heart-broken wail,
And the mother bent low o'er the prostrate child.

LYON.

SING, bird, on green Missouri's plain,
  The saddest song of sorrow;
Drop tears, O clouds, in gentlest rain
  Ye from the winds can borrow;
Breathe out, ye winds, your softest sigh,
  Weep flowers, in dewy splendor,
For him who knew well how to die,
  But never to surrender.

Up rose serene the August sun,
  Upon that day of glory;
Up curled from musket and from gun
  The war-cloud gray and hoary;
It gathered like a funeral pall,
  Now broken and now blended,
Where rang the buffalo's angry call,
  And rank with rank contended.

Four thousand men, as brave and true
  As e'er went forth in daring,

Upon the foe that morning threw
  The strength of their despairing.
They feared not death, — men bless the field
  That patriot soldiers die on;
Fair Freedom's cause was sword and shield, —
  And at their head was Lyon!

Their leader's troubled soul looked forth
  From eyes of troubled brightness;
Sad soul! the burden of the North
  Had pressed out all its lightness.
He gazed upon the unequal fight,
  His ranks all rent and gory,
And felt the shadows close like night
  Round his career of glory.

"General, come, lead us!" loud the cry
  From a brave band was ringing, —
"Lead us, and we will stop, or die,
  That battery's awful singing."
He spurred to where his heroes stood,
  Twice wounded, — no wound knowing, —
The fire of battle in his blood
  And on his forehead glowing.

Oh, cursed for aye that traitor's hand,
  And cursed that aim so deadly,

Which smote the bravest of the land,
  And dyed his bosom redly!
Serene he lay while past him pressed
  The battle's furious billow,
As calmly as a babe may rest
  Upon its mother's pillow.

So Lyon died! and well may flowers
  His place of burial cover,
For never had this land of ours
  A more devoted lover.
Living, his country was his bride,
  His life he gave her dying, —
Life, fortune, love, — he naught denied
  To her and to her sighing.

Rest, Patriot, in thy hill-side grave,
  Beside her form who bore thee!
Long may the land thou died'st to save
  Her bannered stars wave o'er thee!
Upon her history's brightest page,
  And on Fame's glowing portal,
She'll write thy grand, heroic page,
  And grave thy name immortal!

H. P.

KEEP STEP WITH THE MUSIC OF UNION.

BY WILLIAM ROSS WALLACE.

KEEP step with the music of Union,
The music our ancestors sung,
When States, like a jubilant chorus,
To beautiful sisterhood sprung:
Oh thus shall their great Constitution,
That guards all the homes of the land,
A mountain of freedom and justice
For millions eternally stand.
North and South, East and West, all unfurling
One banner alone o'er the sod;
One voice from America swelling
In worship of Liberty's God!

Keep step with the music of Union!
What grandeur its Flag has unrolled
For the loyal, a star-lighted Heaven;
For traitors, a storm in each fold!
The glorious shade of Mount Vernon
Still points to each patriot's grave;
Still cries, "O'er the coming long ages
That banner of Bunker Hill wave!"
North and South, etc.

Keep step with the music of Union!
  The forests have sunk at its sound;
The pioneer's brow been with triumph
  And labor's broad opulence crowned.
O yet shall all rude giant forces
  Of Nature be chained to our cars,
And States that have madly seceded
  Return to the Stripes and the Stars.
    North and South, etc.

Keep step with the music of Union!
  'T is thus we shall nourish the light
Our fathers lit for the chained nations
  That darkle in Tyranny's night.
The blood of the whole world is with us,
  O'er ocean by oligarchs hurled;
And they who would dare to attack us
  Shall sink with the wrath of a world.
    North and South, etc.

"Keep step with the music of Union!"
  So LINCOLN, the glorious, cries,
  (While SCOTT, the majestic, replies,)
The flames of the patriot flashing
  Like lightnings of Heaven from his eyes;
Red wrath on all *Copperhead* villains
  Who dare trail their blasphemous slime

On Loyalty's thrice-sacred flowers,
  That WASHINGTON sowed in our clime.
    North and South, etc.

"Keep step with the music of Union!"
  Hear WEBB, the great ship-builder, shout,
While from his grand "Dunderberg's" armor
  The hammers ring choruses out.
"Down, down with the South's slaving pirates
  Beneath the fierce rams of the Free:
Our flag of DECATUR and PORTER
  Shall yet float the Flag of the Sea!"
    North and South, etc.

"Keep step with the music of Union!"
  America's true women cry;
They know 'tis the sweetest commandment
  God ever glowed down from His sky.
O still by home's altars they sing it,
  Our mothers and daughters divine;
And still lead their sons and their fathers
  To Union's blest *National* shrine.
    North and South, etc.

Keep step with the music of Union!
  All traitors shall sink at its sound,
But patriots march on to Heaven,

With soul-saving harmony crowned.
Then, cheer for the Past with its glory;
For the resolute Present hurrah;
And shout for the starry-browed Future,
With Virtue and Freedom and Law.
North and South, East and West, all unfurling
One Banner alone o'er the sod;
One voice from AMERICA swelling
In worship of Liberty's God!

THE SOLDIER'S DREAM OF HOME.

BY CAROLINE A. MASON.

YOU have put the children to bed, Alice, —
Maud and Willie and Rose; —
They have lisped their sweet "Our Father,"
And sunk to their night's repose.
Did they think of me, dear Alice?
Did they think of me, and say,
"God bless him, and God bless him!
Dear father, far away?"

Oh, my very heart grows sick, Alice,
I long so to behold

Rose, with her pure, white forehead,
  And Maud, with her curls of gold;
And Willie, so gay and sprightly,
  So merry and full of glee;
Oh, my heart *yearns* to enfold ye,
  My "smiling group of three!"

I can bear the noisy day, Alice;
  The camp life, gay and wild,
Shuts from my yearning bosom
  The thoughts of wife and child:
But when the night is round me,
  And under its strong beams
I gather my cloak about me,
  I dream such long, sad dreams!

I think of the pale young wife, Alice,
  Who looked up in my face
When the drum beat at evening,
  And called me to my place.
I think of the three sweet birdlings
  Left in the dear home-nest,
And my soul is sick with longings
  That will not be at rest.

Oh, when will the war be over, Alice!
  Oh, when shall I behold

Rose, with her pure, white forehead,
  And Maud, with her curls of gold;
And Will, so gay and sprightly,
  So merry and full of glee,
And, more than all, the dear wife
  Who bore my babes to me?

God guard and keep you all, Alice;
  God guard and keep me, too;
For if only one were missing,
  What would the other do?
Oh, when will the war be over,
  And when shall I behold
Those whom I love so dearly,
  Safe in the dear home-fold?

THE RESPONSE.

I HAVE put the children to bed, Harry, —
  Rose and Willie and Maud; —
They have sung their hymns together,
  And whispered their prayer to God.
Then Rose said, gently smiling,
  "Come, Willie and Maud, now say,
God bless the dear, sweet father, —
  Father so far away!"

And such a glad trust arose, Harry,
In this sad heart of mine,
For I felt that God would keep you
Safe in His hand divine.
And I kissed their pure, young foreheads,
And said, " He is over all !
He counteth the hair of your heads, darlings,
And noteth the sparrow's fall."

Then I sung them to their sleep, Harry,
With hymns all trust and love,
And I knew that God was listening
From His gracious throne above.
And since that calm, sweet evening,
I have felt so happy, dear !
And so have the children, Harry ;
They seem to know no fear.

They talk of your coming home, Harry,
As something sure to be ;
I list to their childish pratings,
Nor care to check their glee.
For oh, 't is a cause so noble,
And you so brave and true ;
And God protects His own, Harry,
And surely will watch o'er you.

So keep up a brave good heart, Harry!
  God willing — and He knows best —
We 'll welcome you, safe and happy,
  Back to the dear home-nest.
And Maud and Rose and Willie
  Shall yet, with a moistened eye,
Give thanks to the dear, good Father,
  While you stand tearful by.

BRING THE HERO HOME.

IN MEMORY OF GEN. E. D. BAKER.

HE fell in the front of battle,
  Where the brave would wish to die,
Rather than bow to the traitor,
  Or humble our banner and fly.
  Giving for all that was given
  Powder and lead and shell;
Front to front with their bravest,
  Undaunted, unconquered, he fell.

  To right and left and before him,
  A myriad host in power,
Earth torn with thundering iron,
  Air rent with a leaden shower;

A river unbridged behind him,
Rolling its angry tide, —
O'erpowered, betrayed, and deserted,
A hero the patriot died.

Died like the world's first martyr
By the rebel hand of Cain,
A victim on Blunder's red altar,
Through others' incompetence slain.
A sacrifice offered by Folly
That tampered with precious life,
By plunging his gallant legion
In cruel and purposeless strife.

He would not flee from the foeman,
Nor shame the heroes he led;
Rather than life by surrender,
Death with his own brave dead.
Facing the rifle and cannon,
Sulphur and sabre and frown,
True to his country and honor,
Our gallant "Gray Eagle" went down.

Gather the dust of the mighty,
Sleeping so quietly there,
Wash out the blotches of crimson
Clotting his silvery hair.

Woe to the traitors whose bullets
Have channelled a path for the stain, —
That eloquent tongue stilled forever,
And shattered that wonderful brain.

Silenced and hushed and frozen,
Tongue and lip and word,
Brave as the spirit of Freedom,
And true as his flashing sword;
Stilled the heart that quailed not
Before them in forum or field,
That alone to Death would surrender,
And only to Destiny yield.

Take from the field where he battled,
Up from the field where he bled,
His dust; let no soil of the traitor
Give grave to our glorious dead.
For Liberty dwelt in his spirit;
And freemen should fashion his grave
Beneath free humanity's banner,
And not the cursed flag of the slave.

So hither, his relics bring hither,
And let him pass gently to rest,
Like Mars when his night march is ended —
Within his loved land of the West;

Where Poesy, chanting in sorrow,
Shall number the glories he won,
And Eloquence, silent and weeping,
Grieves for her favorite son.

Where comes the voice of the West wind,
From the unmanacled sea,
Free as his chain-spurning spirit,
Let his last dwelling-place be.
Heaven's bright sentinels guarding,
Types of his soul's clear flame,
His requiem chanted by Ocean,
Undying and grand as his fame.

San Francisco, Cal. F. S.

A BATTLE HYMN.

BY GEORGE H. BOKER.

GOD, to Thee we humbly bow,
With hand unarmed and naked brow;
Musket, lance, and sheathed sword
At Thy feet we lay, O Lord!
Gone is all the soldier's boast
In the valor of the host:
Kneeling here, we do our most.

Of ourselves we nothing know:
Thou, and Thou alone canst show,
By the favor of Thy hand,
Who has drawn the guilty brand.
If our foemen have the right,
Show Thy judgment in our sight
Through the fortunes of the fight!

If our cause be pure and just,
Nerve our courage with Thy trust:
Scatter, in Thy bitter wrath,
All who cross the nation's path:
May the baffled traitors fly,
As the vapors from the sky
When Thy raging winds are high!

God of mercy, some must fall
In Thy holy cause. Not all
Hope to sing the victor's lay,
When the sword is laid away.
Brief will be the prayers then said;
Falling at Thy altar dead,
Take the sacrifice, instead.

Now, O God! once more we rise,
Marching on beneath Thy eyes;
And we draw the sacred sword

In Thy name and at Thy word.
May our spirits clearly see
Thee, through all that is to be,
In defeat or victory.

OUR WOUNDED.

BY C. K. TUCKERMAN.

AS loftier rise the ocean's heaving crests,
Ere they sink, tempest-driven, on the strand;
So do these hearts and freedom-beating breasts,
Sublimed by suffering, fall upon our land.

Wounded! O sweet-lipped word! for on the page
Of this strange history, all these scars shall be
The hieroglyphics of a valiant age,
Deep writ in Freedom's blood-red mystery.

What though your fate sharp agony reveals!
What though the mark of brothers' blows you bear!
The breath of your oppression upward steals,
Like incense from crushed spices into air.

Freedom lies listening, nor as yet averts
The battle horrors of these months' slow length;

But as she listens, silently she girts
  More close, more firm, the armor of her strength.

Then deem them not as lost, these bitter days,
  Nor those which yet in anguish must be spent
Far from loved skies and home's peace-moving ways,
  For these are not the losses you lament.

It is the glory that your country bore
  Which you would rescue from a living grave;
It is the unity that once she wore
  Which your true hearts are yearning still to save.

Despair not: *it is written!* Though the eye,
  Red with its watching, can no future scan,
The glow of triumph yet shall flush the sky,
  And God redeem the ruin made by man.

"AT EVENING TIME IT SHALL BE LIGHT."

OUR Nation's Sun was clouded o'er
  When erst he rose at morn;
But soon those beams were hid no more,
  Afar the clouds were borne.

We for awhile enjoyed his rays,
    In all their noontide power;
Now once again is hid that blaze
    In this our darkest hour.
But Freedom's sky shall yet be bright:
" At Evening time it shall be light."

The Sun of Liberty shall ne'er
    In clouds and darkness set;
Her sons are brave, — they know no fear, —
    And God is with us yet.
We know whatever may betide,
    Be it for good or ill,
It is in mercy He doth chide,
    His arm is pow'rful still.
Then strike! for God and for the Right:
" At Evening time it shall be light."

C. F.

TRUMPET SONG.

BY OLIVER WENDELL HOLMES.

THE battle-drum's loud rattle is rending the air,
The troopers all are mounted, their sabres are
    bare;

The guns are unlimbered, the bayonets shine,
Hark! hark! 't is the trumpet-call! wheel into line!
Ta ra! ta ta ta!
Trum trum, tra ra ra ra!
Beat drums and blow trumpets!
Hurrah, boys, hurrah!

March onward, soldiers, onward, the strife is begun,
Loud bellowing rolls the boom of the black-throated gun;
The rifles are cracking, the torn banners toss,
The sabres are clashing, the bayonets cross.
Ta ra, etc.

Down with the leaguing liars, the traitors to their trust,
Who trampled the fair charter of Freedom in dust!
They falter — they waver — they scatter — they run —
The field is our own, and the battle is won!
Ta ra, etc.

God save our mighty people and prosper our cause!
We 're fighting for our nation, our land, and our laws!

Though tyrants may hate us, their threats we defy,
And drum-beat and trumpet shall peal our reply!
Ta ra! ta ta ta!
Beat drums and blow trumpets!
Trum trum, tra ra ra ra!
Hurrah, boys, hurrah!

PUT IT THROUGH.

COME Freemen of the land,
Come meet the last demand!
Here 's a piece of work in hand:
Put it through!

Here 's a log across the way,
We have stumbled on all day,
Here 's a ploughshare in the clay:
Put it through!

Here 's a country that 's half free,
And it waits for you and me,
To say what it's fate shall be:
Put it through!

While one traitor thought remains,
While one spot its banner stains,
One link of all its chains :
Put it through !

Hear our brothers in the field,
Steel your swords as their's are steeled,
Learn to wield the arms they wield :
Put it through !

Lock the shop and lock the store,
Chalk this upon the door,
" We 've enlisted for the War ! "
Put it through !

For the Birthrights yet unsold,
For the History yet untold,
For the Future yet unrolled,
Put it through !

Lest our children point with shame,
On the father's dastard fame,
Who gave up a nation's name,
Put it through !

Father Abram, hear us cry,
" We can follow, we can die."

Lead your children then, and try
Put it through!

Here's a work of God half done,
Here's the kingdom of His Son,
With its triumphs just begun:
Put it through!

Father Abram, that man thrives
Who with every weapon strives;
Use our twenty million lives!
Put it through!

'Tis to you the Trust is given!
'Tis by you the Bolt is driven!
By the very God of Heaven,
Drive it through!

ROLL CALL.

BY N. G. SHEPHERD.

"CORPORAL Green!" the orderly cried;
"Here!" was the answer, loud and clear,
From the lips of a soldier who stood near;
And "Here!" was the word the next replied.

"Cyrus Drew!" — then a silence fell, —
  This time no answer followed the call;
  Only his rear-man had seen him fall,
Killed or wounded he could not tell.

There they stood in the failing light,
  These men of battle, with grave, dark looks,
  As plain to be read as open books;
While slowly gathered the shade of night.

The fern on the hill-sides were splashed with blood,
  And down in the corn, where the poppies grew,
  Wore redder stains than the poppies knew;
And crimson-dyed as the river's flood.

For the foe had crossed from the other side
  That day, in the face of a murderous fire
  That swept them down in its terrible ire;
And their life-blood went to color the tide.

"Herbert Cline!" — At the call there came
  Two stalwart soldiers into the line,
  Bearing between them this Herbert Cline,
Wounded and bleeding, to answer his name.

"Ezra Kerr!" — and a voice answered "Here!"
  "Hiram Kerr!" but no man replied:

They were brothers, these two; the sad wind sighed,
And a shudder crept through the corn-field near.

"Ephraim Deane!" — then a soldier spoke:
"Deane carried our regiment's colors," he said,
"When our ensign was shot; I left him dead,
Just after the enemy wavered and broke.

"Close to the roadside his body lies;
I paused a moment and gave him to drink;
He murmured his mother's name, I think;
And Death came with it and closed his eyes."

'T was a victory — yes: but it cost us dear;
For that company's roll, when called at night,
Of a hundred men who went into the fight,
Numbered but twenty that answered "*Here!*"

"PICCIOLA."

IT was a sergeant old and gray,
Well singed and bronzed from siege and pillage,
Went tramping in an army's wake,
Along the turnpike of the village.

For days and nights the winding host
  Had through the little place been marching,
And ever loud the rustics cheered,
  Till ev'ry throat was hoarse and parching.

The squire and farmer, maid and dame,
  All took the sight's electric stirring,
And hats were waved, and staves were sung,
  And 'kerchiefs white were countless whirling.

They only saw a gallant show
  Of heroes stalwart under banners,
And in the fierce heroic glow
  'T was theirs to yield but wild hosannahs.

The sergeant heard the shrill hurrahs,
  Where he behind in step was keeping;
But glancing down beside the road
  He saw a little maid sit weeping.

"And how is this?" he gruffly said,
  A moment pausing to regard her;
"Why weepest thou, my little chit?"
  And then she only cried the harder.

"And how is this, my little chit?"
  The sturdy trooper straight repeated, —

"When all the village cheers us on,
That you, in tears, apart are seated?

"We march two hundred thousand strong!
And that 's a sight, my baby beauty,
To quicken silence into song,
And glorify the soldier's duty."

"It 's very, very grand, I know,"
The little maid gave soft replying;
"And father, mother, brother, too,
All say 'hurrah' while I am crying.

"But think — O Mr. Soldier, think,
How many little sisters' brothers
Are going all away to fight,
Who may be *killed*, as well as others!"

"Why, bless thee, child," the sergeant said,
His brawny hand her curls caressing,
"'T is left for little ones like you
To find that war 's not all a blessing."

And "bless thee!" once again he cried;
Then cleared his throat and looked indignant,
And marched away with wrinkled brow
To stop the straggling tear benignant.

And still the ringing shouts went up
  From doorway, thatch, and fields of tillage;
The pall behind the standard seen
  By one alone, of all the village.

The oak and cedar bend and writhe
  When roars the wind through gap and braken;
But 't is the tenderest reed of all
  That trembles first when earth is shaken.

MOVE ON THE COLUMNS.

BY W. D. GALLAGHER.

I.

MOVE on the columns! Why delay?
  Our soldiers sicken in their camps:
  The summer heats, the autumn damps,
Have sapp'd their vigor, day by day;
  And now the winter comes apace,
  With death-chills in its cold embrace,
More fatal than the battle fray.

II.

Move on the columns! Hesitate
  No longer what to plan or do:
  Our cause is good — our men are true —

This fight is for the Flag, the State,
  The Union, and the hopes of man:
  And Right will end what Wrong began,
For God the Right will vindicate.

III.

Move on the columns! If the land
  Is lock'd by winter, take the sea;
  No possible barrier can be
So fatal to a rightful stand,
  As wavering purpose when at bay.
  This way or THAT — "at once! to-day!"
Were worth ten thousand men at hand.

IV.

Move on the columns! With the sweep
  Of eagles let them strike the foe;
  The hurricane lays the forest low:
Momentum wings the daring leap
  That clears the chasm: the lightning stroke
  Shivers the wind-defying oak;
The earthquake rocks the eternal steep.

V.

Move on the columns! Why have sprung
  Our myriad hosts from hill and plain?
  Leaving the sickle in the grain, —

Closing the harvest hymn half sung, —
  Half filled the granary and the mow, —
  Unturn'd the sod, untouch'd the plough, —
Scythes rusting where they last were swung.

VI.

Move on the columns! They are here
  To found anew a people's faith,
  To save from treason and from death
A nation which they all revere;
  And on each manly brow is set
  A purpose such as never yet
Was thwarted when, as now, sincere.

VII.

Move on the columns! Earth contains
  No guerdon for the good and free
  Like that which bless'd our Liberty:
And while its banner still remains
  The symbol of united power,
  Nor man nor fiend can tell the hour
In which its star-lit glory wanes.

VIII.

Move on the columns strong and bright!
  Strike down the sacrilegious hands
  That clutch and wield the battle brands

Which menace with their Wrong our Right,
Words now are wasted — glittering steel
Alone can make the last appeal:
They 've will'd it so — and we must fight.

IX.

Move on the columns! If they go
By ways they had not thought to take,
To fields we had not meant to make;
Or if they bring unthought-of woe,
Let that which woke the fiery wrath
Fall, scorn'd and blackening in its path.
Not man, but God, may stay the blow.
Move on the columns!

LANDER.

BY THOMAS BAILEY ALDRICH.

CLOSE his bleak eyes — they shall no more
Flash victory where the cannon roar;
And lay the battered sabre at his side,
(His to the last, for so he would have died!)
Though he no more may pluck from out its sheath
The sinewy lightning that dealt traitors death.
Lead the worn war-horse by the pluméd bier —
Even his horse, now he is dead, is dear!

Take him, New England, now his work is done.
He fought the good fight valiantly — and won.
Speak of his daring. This man held his blood
Cheaper than water for the nation's good.
Rich Mountain, Fairfax, Romney, — he was there.
Speak of him gently, of his mien, his air;
How true he was, how his strong heart could bend
With sorrow, like a woman's, for a friend:
Intolerant of every mean desire:
Ice where he liked not; where he loved, all fire.

Take him, New England, gently. Other days,
Peaceful and prosperous, shall give him praise.
How will our children's children breathe his name,
Bright on the shadowy muster-roll of fame!
Take him, New England, gently; you can fold
No purer patriot in your soft brown mould.

So, on New England's bosom, let him lie,
Sleeping awhile — as if the Good could die!

GENTLY! GENTLY!

Among the wounded was a young soldier whose limbs were fearfully shattered. Though evidently in intense pain, he uttered no cry; but, as the carriers raised the "stretcher" he was on, he whispered, "Gently! gently!"

THOUGH he neither sighs nor groans,
Death is busy with his bones:
Bear him o'er the jutting stones
Gently! gently!

Sisters, faithful to your vow,
Swathe his limbs and cool his brow:
Peace! his soul is passing now
Gently! gently!

He has fallen in the strife!
Tell it to his widowed wife,
And to her who gave him life,
Gently! gently!

Loudly praise the brave who gem
With their blood our diadem:
And their faults — oh, speak of *them*
Gently! gently!

NOT YET.

BY WILLIAM CULLEN BRYANT.

O COUNTRY, marvel of the earth!
  O realm to sudden greatness grown!
The age that gloried in thy birth,
  Shall it behold thee overthrown?
Shall traitors lay that greatness low?
No, Land of Hope and Blessing, No!

And we who wear thy glorious name,
  Shall we, like cravens, stand apart,
When those whom thou hast trusted aim
  The death-blow at thy generous heart?
Forth goes the battle-cry, and lo!
Hosts rise in harness, shouting, No!

And they who founded, in our land,
  The power that rules from sea to sea,
Bled they in vain, or vainly planned
  To leave their country great and free?
Their sleeping ashes, from below,
Send up the thrilling murmur, No!

Knit they the gentle ties which long
  These sister States were proud to wear,

And forged the kindly links so strong
  For idle hands in sport to tear, —
For scornful hands aside to throw?
No, by our fathers' memory, No!

Our humming marts, our iron ways,
  Our wind-tossed woods on mountain crest,
The hoarse Atlantic, with his bays,
  The calm, broad Ocean of the West,
And Mississippi's torrent flow,
And loud Niagara, answer, No!

Not yet the hour is nigh, when they
  Who deep in Eld's dim twilight sit,
Earth's ancient kings, shall rise and say,
  "Proud country, welcome to the pit!
So soon art thou, like us, brought low?"
No, sullen groups of shadows, No!

For now, behold the arm that gave
  The victory in our fathers' day,
Strong, as of old, to guard and save, —
  That mighty arm which none can stay, —
On clouds above and fields below,
Writes, in men's sight, the answer, No!

MARCH ALONG.

BY GEORGE H. BOKER.

SOLDIERS are we from the mountain and valley,
  Soldiers are we from the hill and the plain;
Under the flag of our fathers we rally;
  Death, for its sake, is but living again.
      Then march along, gay and strong,
      March to battle with a song!
        March, march along!

We have a history told of our nation,
  We have a name that must never go down;
Heroes achieved it through toil and privation;
  Bear it on, bright with its ancient renown!
      Then march along, etc.

Who that shall dare say the flag waving o'er us,
  Which floated in glory from Texas to Maine,
Must fall, where our ancestors bore it before us,
  Writes his own fate on the roll of the slain.
      Then march along, etc.

Look at it, traitors, and blush to behold it!
  Quail as it flashes its stars in the sun!

Think you a hand in the nation will fold it,
  While there 's a hand that can level a gun?
      Then march along, etc.

Carry it onward till victory earn it
  The rights it once owned in the land of the free;
Then, in God's name, in our fury we 'll turn it
  Full on the treachery over the sea!
      Then march along, etc.

England shall feel what a vengeance the liar
  Stores in the bosom he aims to deceive;
England shall feel how God's truth can inspire;
  England shall feel it, but only to grieve.
      Then march along, etc.

Peace shall unite us again and forever,
  Though thousands lie cold in the graves of these wars;
Those who survive them shall never prove, never,
  False to the flag of the stripes and the stars!
      Then march along, gay and strong,
      March to the battle with a song!
        March, march along!

THE UNION—RIGHT OR WRONG.

BY GEORGE. P. MORRIS.

I.

IN Freedom's name our blades we draw,
  She arms us for the fight!
For country, government, and law,
  For Liberty and Right.
The Union must — shall be preserved,
  Our flag still o'er us fly!
That cause our hearts and hands has nerved,
  And we will do or die.

CHORUS.

Then come, ye hardy volunteers,
  Around our standard throng,
And pledge man's hope of coming years, —
  The Union, — right or wrong!
The Union — right or wrong — inspires
  The burden of our song;
It was the glory of our sires —
  The Union, — right or wrong!

II.

It is the duty of us all
  To check rebellion's sway;

To rally at the nation's call,
  And we that voice obey!
Then like a band of brothers go,
  A hostile league to break,
To rout a spoil-encumber'd foe,
  And what is ours, retake.

CHORUS.

So come, ye hardy volunteers,
  Around our standard throng,
And pledge man's hope of coming years, —
  The Union, — right or wrong!
The Union — right or wrong — inspires
  The burden of our song;
It was the glory of our sires —
  The Union, — right or wrong!

GONE TO THE WAR.

BY HORATIO ALGER, JR.

MY Charlie has gone to the war,
  My Charlie so brave and tall;
He left his plough in the furrow
  And flew at his country's call.
May God in safety keep him,
  My precious boy — my all.

My heart is pining to see him,
  I miss him every day;
My heart is weary with waiting,
  And sick of the long delay.
But I know his country needs him,
  And I could not bid him stay.

I remember how his face flushed,
  And how his color came,
When the flash from the guns of Sumter
  Lit the whole land with flame,
And darkened our country's banner
  With the crimson hue of shame.

"Mother," he said, then faltered, —
  I felt his mute appeal;
I paused, — if you are a mother,
  You know what mothers feel,
When called to yield their dear ones
  To the cruel bullet and steel.

My heart stood still for a moment,
  Struck with a mighty woe;
A faint of death came o'er me, —
  I am a mother, you know, —
But I sternly checked my weakness,
  And firmly bade him "Go."

Wherever the fight is fiercest
  I know that my boy will be;
Wherever the need is sorest
  Of the stout arms of the free,
May he prove as true to his country
  As he has been true to me!

My home is lonely without him,
  My heart bereft of joy,—
The thought of him who has left me
  My constant, sad employ;
But God has been good to the mother;
  She shall not blush for her boy.

TO THE UNITED STATES.

BY MAYNE REID.

OH! land of my longings, beyond the Atlantic,
  What horrible dream has disturbed thy repose?
What demon has driven thy citizens frantic,—
  A grief to their friends, and a joy to their foes?

Is it true they are arming to kill one another?
  That sire and son are in hostile array?
That brother is baring his blade against brother,—
  Each madly preparing the other to slay?

Is it true the star-banner, so dear to the sight
Of all freemen, may fall by a factionist's blow, —
That banner I've borne through the midst of the fight,
Side by side with my sons, as we charged on the foe?

I would not, I will not, I can not believe it!
Oh! rally around it, and stand by the staff!
Or the children of men will have reason to grieve it,
And the tyrants of men will exultingly laugh.

Ay, sure would the kings and the princes of earth
Greet the fall of thy flag with a joyous "hurrah!"
Even now, scarce suppressing demoniac mirth,
They would hail thy decadence with fiendish "Ha, ha!"

And he who would help them to win their foul game,
Whether Northern or Southern, — no matter which claims him, —
Be a brand on his brow, and a blight on his fame,
And scorn on the lip of the humblest who name him!

Be palsied the arm that draws sword fratricidal!
May the steel of the traitor be broken in two!
May his maiden betrothed, on the morn of his bridal,
Prove faithless to him as he has been to you!

United, no power 'neath heaven can shake thee, —
No purple-robed despot e'er smile on thy shame;
Asunder, like reeds they will bruise thee and break thee,
And waste thee as flax in the pitiless flame.

Woe, woe to the world, if this fatal division
Should ever arise in the ranks of the free;
Oh, brother! avoid, then, the fearful collision,
And millions unborn will sing praises to thee!

BATTLE-ANTHEM.

BY JOHN NEAL.

UP, Christian Warrior, up! I hear
The trumpet of the North
Sounding the charge!
Fathers and Sons! — to horse!
Fling the Old Standard forth,
Blazing and large!

And now I hear the heavy tramp
Of nations on the march,
Silent as death!
A slowly gathering host,
Like clouds o'er yonder arch,
Holding their breath!

Our great blue sky is overcast;
And stars are dropping out,
Through smoke and flame!
Hailstones and coals of fire!
Now comes the battle-shout;
Jehovah's name!

And now the rebel pomp! To prayer!
Look to your stirrups, men!
Yonder rides Death!
Now with a whirlwind-sweep!
Empty their saddles when
Hot comes their breath!

As through the midnight forest tears
With trumpeting and fire
A thunder-blast;
So, Reapers! tear your way
Through yonder camp, until you hear
"It is enough! Put up thy sword!

O, Angel of the Lord!
My wrath is past!"

BOY BRITTAN.

BY FORCEYTHE WILLSON.

I.

BOY Brittan — only a lad — a fair-haired boy — sixteen,
In his uniform!
Into the storm — into the roaring jaws of grim Fort Henry —
Boldly bears the Federal flotilla —
Into the battle-storm!

II.

Boy Brittan is Master's Mate aboard of the Essex —
There he stands buoyant and eager-eyed,
By the brave Captain's side;
Ready to do and dare — aye, aye sir! always ready —
In his country's uniform!
Boom! Boom! and now the flag-boat sweeps, and now the Essex,
Into the battle storm!

III.

Boom! Boom! till River and Fort and Field are
overclouded
By battle's breath; then from the Fort a gleam
And a crashing gun, and the Essex is wrapt and
shrouded
In a scalding cloud of steam!

IV.

But victory! victory!
Unto God all praise be ever rendered,
Unto God all praise and glory be!
See, Boy Brittan; see, Boy, see!
They strike! Hurrah! the Fort has just surren-
dered!
Shout! Shout! my Boy, my warrior Boy!
And wave your cap and clap your hands for joy!
Cheer answer cheer and bear the cheer about —
Hurrah! Hurrah! for the fiery Fort is ours;
And "Victory!" "Victory!" "Victory!"
Is the shout.
Shout — for the fiery Fort, and the Field, and the
day are ours —
The day is ours — thanks to the brave endeavor
Of heroes, Boy, like thee!
The day is ours — the day is ours!
Glory and deathless love to all who shared with thee,

And bravely endured and dared with thee —
The day is ours — the day is ours —
Forever!
Glory and Love for one and all; but — but — for thee —
Home! Home! a happy "Welcome — welcome home" for thee!
And kisses of love for thee —
And a Mother's happy, happy tears, and a virgin's bridal wreath of flowers —
For thee!

V.

Victory! Victory!
But suddenly wrecked and wrapt in seething steam, the Essex
Slowly drifted out of the battle's storm;
Slowly, slowly — down — laden with the dead and the dying;
And there, at the Captain's feet, among the dead and the dying,
The shot-marred form of a beautiful Boy is lying —
There in his uniform!

VI.

Laurels and tears for thee, Boy,
Laurels and tears for thee!

Laurels of light, moist with the precious dew
  Of the inmost heart of the Nation's loving heart,
And blest by the balmy breath of the Beautiful and
      the True;

Moist — moist with the luminous breath of the
      singing spheres
        And the Nation's starry tears!
And tremble-touched by the pulse-like gush and
      start
Of the universal music of the heart,
        And all deep sympathy!
Laurels and tears for thee, Boy,
        Laurels and tears for thee —
Laurels of light, and tears of love, forevermore —
        For thee!

VII.

And laurels of Light, and tears of Truth,
        And the Mantle of Immortality;
And the flowers of Love and immortal Youth,
And the tender heart-tokens of all true ruth —
        And the Everlasting Victory!
    And the breath and bliss of Liberty,
    And the loving kiss of Liberty;
And the welcoming light of heavenly eyes,
    And the over-calm of God's canopy;

And the infinite love-span of the skies
That cover the Valleys of Paradise —
  For all of the brave who rest with thee;
  And for one and all who died with thee,
  And now sleep side by side with thee ;
And for every one who lives and dies,
  On the solid land or the heaving sea,
      Dear warrior-boy — like thee.

VIII.

      O, the Victory — the Victory
      Belongs to thee!
God ever keeps the brightest crown for such as thou —
      He gives it now to thee!
O Young and Brave, and early and thrice blest —
      Thrice, thrice, thrice blest!
Thy Country turns once more to kiss thy youthful brow,
  And takes thee — gently — gently to her breast;
And whispers lovingly, "God bless thee — bless thee now —
      My darling, thou shalt rest!"

"THE LAST BROADSIDE."

BY ELIZABETH T. PORTER BEACH.

The following lines were written upon hearing of the heroism of the crew of the "Frigate Cumberland," in the engagement at "Hampton Roads," who bravely fired a last "Broadside" while their ship was sinking, in compliance with the order of their Commanding Officer, the gallant hero, Lieutenant Morris.

"*Shall we give them a Broadside as she goes?*"

SHALL we give them a Broadside, my boys, as she goes?
Shall we send yet another to TELL,
In iron-tongued words, to Columbia's foes,
How bravely her sons say Farewell?

Ay! what though we sink 'neath the turbulent wave,
'T is with DUTY and RIGHT at the helm;
And over the form should the fierce waters rave,
No tide can the spirit o'erwhelm!

For swift o'er the billows of Charon's dark stream
We 'll pass to the Immortal shore,
Where the "waters of life" in brilliancy beam,
And the pure float in peace evermore!

Shall we give them a Broadside once more, my brave men?
"Ay! Ay!" rose the full, earnest cry;
"A Broadside! A Broadside! we'll give them again!
Then for God and the Right nobly die."

"Haste! Haste!"—for amid all that battling din
Comes a gurgling sound fraught with fear,
As swift flowing waters pour rushingly in;
Up! Up! till her portholes they near.

No blenching!—no faltering!—still fearless all seem;
Each man firm to duty doth bide;
A flash! and a "Broadside!" a shout! a careen!
And the Cumberland sinks 'neath the tide!

The "Star Spangled Banner" still floating above!
As a beacon upon the dark wave!
Our Ensign of Glory, proud streaming in love,
O'er the tomb of the "Loyal and Brave!"

Bold hearts! mighty spirits! "tried gold" of our land!
A halo of glory your meed!
All honored, the noble-souled Cumberland band!
So true in Columbia's need!

A CALL FOR TRUE MEN.

BY ROBERT LOWELL.

UP to battle! Up to battle!
All we love is saved or lost!
Workshop's hum and wayside's tattle,
Off! This thing the life may cost.
Come, for your country! For all dear things, come!
Come to the roll of the rallying drum!

You have seen the spring-swollen river
Hurling torrent, ice and wreck!
You have felt the strong pier quiver
Like a tempest-shaken deck: —
Many a stout heart, quick hand, and eye,
Broke the water's mad strength, and it went by.

Look on this mad, threatening torrent,
Tumbling on, with blood and death!
Will we see our bulwarks war-rent?
Never! Snatch a stronger breath:
Here is good man's work! Break through, and through!
What matters hardship, or danger, to you?

What were death to any true man,
  If the cause be true and high?
Beastly might quails under human
  Looking calmly in its eye.
Come! with your fearless strength break yonder ranks!
God's blessing! glory! and evermore thanks!

VOYAGE OF THE GOOD SHIP UNION.

BY OLIVER WENDELL HOLMES.

'TIS midnight: through my troubled dream
  Loud wails the tempest's cry;
Before the gale, with tattered sail,
  A ship goes plunging by.
What name? Where bound? — The rocks around
  Repeat the loud halloo.
— The good ship Union, Southward bound:
  God help her and her crew!

And is the old flag flying still
  That o'er your fathers flew,
With bands of white and rosy light,
  And field of starry blue?
— Ay! look aloft! its folds full oft
  Have braved the roaring blast,

And still shall fly when from the sky
  This black typhoon has past!

Speak, pilot of the storm-tost bark!
  May I thy perils share?
— Oh landsmen, these are fearful seas
  The brave alone may dare!
— Nay, ruler of the rebel deep,
  What matters wind or wave?
The rocks that wreck your reeling deck
  Will leave me nought to save!

Oh, landsman, art thou false or true?
  What sign hast thou to show?
— The crimson stains from loyal veins
  That hold my heart-blood's flow!
— Enough! what more shall honor claim?
  I know the sacred sign;
Above thy head our flag shall spread,
  Our ocean path be thine!

The bark sails on: the Pilgrims' Cape
  Lies low along her lee,
Whose headland crooks its anchor flukes
  To lock the shore and sea.
No treason here! it cost too dear
  To win this barren realm!

And true and free the hands must be
That hold the whaler's helm!

Still on! Manhattan's narrowing bay
No Rebel cruiser scars;
Her waters feel no pirate's keel
That flaunts the fallen stars!
— But watch the light on yonder height, —
Ay, pilot, have a care!
Some lingering cloud in mist may shroud
The Capes of Delaware!

Say, pilot, what this fort may be
Whose sentinels look down
From moated walls that show the sea
Their deep embrasures' frown?
The Rebel host claims all the coast,
But these are friends, we know,
Whose footprints spoil the "sacred soil,"
And this is? —— Fort Monroe!

The breakers roar, — how bears the shore?
— The traitorous wreckers' hands
Have quenched the blaze that poured its rays
Along the Hatteras sands.
— Ha! say not so! I see its glow!
Again the shoals display

The beacon light that shines by night,
  The Union Stars by day!

The good ship flies to milder skies,
  The wave more gently flows;
The softening breeze wafts o'er the seas
  The breath of Beaufort's rose.
What fold is this the sweet winds kiss,
  Fair-striped and many-starred,
Whose shadow palls the orphaned walls,
  The twins of Beauregard?

What! heard you not Port Royal's doom?
  How the black war-ships came
And turned the Beaufort roses' bloom
  To redder wreaths of flame?
How from Rebellion's broken reed
  We saw his emblem fall,
As soon his cursèd poison-weed
  Shall drop from Sumter's wall?

On! on! Pulaski's iron hail
  Falls harmless on Tybee!
Her topsails feel the freshening gale, —
  She strikes the open sea;
She rounds the point, she threads the keys
  That guard the Land of Flowers,

And rides at last where firm and fast
  Her own Gibraltar towers!

The good ship Union's voyage is o'er,
  At anchor safe she swings,
And loud and clear with cheer on cheer
  Her joyous welcome rings:
Hurrah! Hurrah! it shakes the wave,
  It thunders on the shore,—
One flag, one land, one heart, one hand,
  One Nation, evermore!

THE BIBLE AND THE SHELL.

BY REV. CHARLES W. DENISON, CHAPLAIN U. S. A.

AT Fredericksburg, when foemen waged
  The battle of the plain,
A soldier, face to face engaged,
  Through smoke and fog and rain,
Knelt down beside his trusty gun,
  Among the shrieking shell,
Nor paused until the day was done,
  And to the earth he fell.

Stretched out upon the trembling ground,
  He bleeding, helpless lay;
His Bible on his breast was found,
  Where his coat was torn away:
A shell had struck the sacred book,
  And shattered it apart;
But there the fragment glanced, and took
  Its leap from off his heart!

A Minie ball came singing, then,
  And lodged in his bosom's flesh;
But he rose alive, among dying men,
  And knelt and fought afresh.
Again this living truth was graved
  On that torn and bloody sod, —
Full many a soldier's life is saved
  By the Holy Book of God.

SONG FOR OUR SOLDIERS.

BY ALICE CARY.

OH! for the Union, boys!
  Ho! for the Union, boys:
Go for the Union, boys,
  Heart, hand, and gun.

Shoulder to shoulder, boys,
Younger and older, boys,
Bolder and bolder, boys,
  Every mother's son!

Where you find the white men,
Union-hating white men,
Ribald rabble white men,
  Let your cannon play.
Where you find the black men,
Union-loving black men,
True and loyal black men,
  Let 'em run away!
Break off their chains, boys!
Strike off their chains, boys!
Knock off their chains, boys,
  And let 'em run away.

Oh! for the Union, boys!
Ho! for the Union, boys:
Go for the Union, boys,
  Heart, hand, and sword.
Shoulder to shoulder, boys,
Bolder and bolder, boys,
Younger and older, boys,
  Trusting in the Lord.

Where you find the white men,
Union-hating white men,
Ribald rabble white men,
  Let your cannon play!
Where you find the black men,
Union-loving black men,
True and loyal black men,
  Let 'em run away.
Break off their chains, boys!
Strike off their chains, boys!
Knock off their chains, boys,
  And let 'em run away!

THE VOLUNTEER.

BY ELBRIDGE JEFFERSON CUTLER.

"AT dawn," he said, "I bid them all farewell,
  To go where bugles call and rifles gleam."
And with the restless thought asleep he fell
    And glided into dream.

A great hot plain from sea to mountain spread,—
  Through it a level river slowly drawn;
He moved with a vast crowd, and at its head
    Streamed banners like the dawn.

There came a blinding flash, a deafening roar,
  And dissonant cries of triumph and dismay;
Blood trickled down the river's reedy shore,
    And with the dead he lay.

The morn broke in upon his solemn dreams,
  And still, with steady pulse and deepening eye,
"Where bugles call," he said, "and rifles gleam,
    I follow, though I die!"

Wise youth! By few is glory's wreath attained;
  But death, or late or soon, awaiteth all.
To fight in Freedom's cause is something gained,—
    And nothing lost, to fall.

THEN AND NOW.

'TWAS the night before Christmas, just one year ago,
In the same little cot slept Nannie and Joe,
While wonderful dreams swarmed through each cunning head
Of the stockings they 'd hung at the sides of their bed.
A very slight creak of the nursery door,

Some slow muffled footsteps across the smooth
floor,
And Pa and Mamma each laden with toys,
Soon filled the wee stockings with numberless joys.
A long look, a fond look at each darling face,
A thought of the morrow their gladness would
grace;
Then on tiptoe retreating, they too sank in slumber,
Surrounded by blessings their lips scarce could
number.

. . . .

'Tis the night before Christmas, and Nannie and
Joe
Are drearily watching the fast falling snow;
Their hearts and their fancies have travelled afar,
After Father, *dear* Father, who 's gone to the war;
And they wonder what need for Christmas to
come,
Since darling Papa cannot spend it at home.
Mamma, dimly seen by the fire-light's glare,
Rocks herself to and fro in *his* favorite chair,
While fears for the present and thoughts of the
past,
Like shadows alternate are over her cast.
The sweet recollection of one year ago,

Lies pure in her heart as does moonlight on snow.
" But where is he now ? " a low, wailing cry,
Wrung by torturing doubt, is the only reply.

. . . .

Upon Rappahannock's memorable shore,
The loved Father sleeps to awaken no more.
One sharp pang in battle, — " *My Children! My Wife!* "
And he fell in the glorious noon of his life.

Oh God of great pity! Whenever death comes,
Be Thou comfort and light in the desolate homes;
May Bethlehem's Christ-child descend like a dove,
And fold little ones 'neath the wings of His love;
And when, in Thy mercy, earth's last links are riven,
Oh, grant a re-union, — a Christmas in Heaven.

N.

THE CUMBERLAND.

BY HENRY W. LONGFELLOW.

AT anchor in Hampton Roads we lay,
On board the Cumberland sloop-of-war;
And at times from the fortress across the bay

The alarm of drums swept past,
Or a bugle-blast
From the camp on shore.

Then far away to the South uprose
A little feather of snow-white smoke,
And we knew that the iron ship of our foes
Was steadily steering its course
To try the force
Of our ribs of oak.

Down upon us heavily runs
Silent and sullen the floating fort;
Then comes a puff of smoke from her guns,
And leaps the terrible death,
With fiery breath,
From each open port.

We are not idle, but send her straight
Defiance back in a full broadside!
As hail rebounds from a roof of slate,
Rebounds our heavier hail
From each iron scale
Of the monster's hide.

"Strike your flag!" the rebel cries,
In his arrogant old plantation strain,

"Never!" our gallant Morris replies;
"It is better to sink than to yield!"
And the whole air pealed
With the cheers of our men.

Then, like a kraken huge and black,
She crushed our ribs in her iron grasp!
Down went the Cumberland all a wrack,
With a sudden shudder of death,
And the cannon's breath
For her dying gasp.

Next morn, as the sun rose over the bay,
Still floated our flag at the mainmast-head.
Lord, how beautiful was Thy day!
Every waft of the air
Was a whisper of prayer,
Or a dirge for the dead.

Ho! brave hearts that went down in the seas,
Ye are at peace in the troubled stream.
Ho! brave land! with hearts like these,
Thy flag, that is rent in twain,
Shall be one again,
And without a seam.

ON THE SHORES OF TENNESSEE.

MOVE my arm-chair, faithful Pompey,
  In the sunshine bright and strong,
For this world is fading, Pompey, —
  Massa won't be with you long;
And I fain would hear the south wind
  Bring once more the sound to me,
Of the wavelets softly breaking
  On the shores of Tennessee.

"Mournful though the ripples murmur,
  As they still the story tell,
How no vessels float the banner
  That I've loved so long and well.
I shall listen to their music,
  Dreaming that again I see
Stars and Stripes on sloop and shallop
  Sailing up the Tennessee.

"And, Pompey, while old Massa's waiting
  For Death's last despatch to come,
If that exiled, starry banner
  Should come proudly sailing home,
You shall greet it, slave no longer; —
  Voice and hand shall both be free

That shout and point to Union colors
  On the waves of Tennessee."

" Massa 's berry kind to Pompey ;
  But ole darkey 's happy here,
Where he 's tended corn and cotton
  For 'ese many a long gone year.
Over yonder Missis' sleeping, —
  No one tends her grave like me ;
Mebbie she would miss the flowers
  She used to love in Tennessee.

" 'Pears like she was watching, Massa —
  If Pompey should beside him stay ;
Mebbie she 'd remember better
  How for him she used to pray ;
Telling him that way up yonder
  White as snow his soul would be,
If he served the Lord of Heaven
  While he lived in Tennessee."

Silently the tears were rolling
  Down the poor old dusky face,
As he stepped behind his master,
  In his long-accustomed place.
Then a silence fell around them,
  As they gazed on rock and tree

Pictured in the placid waters
  Of the rolling Tennessee.

Master, dreaming of the battle
  Where he fought by Marion's side,
When he bid the haughty Tarleton
  Stoop his lordly crest of pride.
Man, remembering how yon sleeper
  Once he held upon his knee,
Ere she loved the gallant soldier,
  Ralph Vervair of Tennessee.

Still the south wind fondly lingers
  'Mid the veteran's silver hair;
Still the bondman close beside him
  Stands behind the old arm-chair.
With his dark-hued hand uplifted,
  Shading eyes, he bends to see
Where the woodland, boldly jutting,
  Turns aside the Tennessee.

Thus he watches cloud-born shadows
  Glide from tree to mountain crest,
Softly creeping, aye and ever
  To the river's yielding breast.
Ha! above the foliage yonder
  Something flutters wild and free!

"Massa! Massa! Hallelujah!
  The flag's come back to Tennessee!"

"Pompey, hold me on your shoulder,
  Help me stand on foot once more,
That I may salute the colors
  As they pass my cabin door;
Here's the paper signed that frees you,
  Give a freeman's shout with me —
'God and Union!' be our watchword
  Evermore in Tennessee."

Then the trembling voice grew fainter,
  And the limbs refused to stand;
One prayer to Jesus — and the soldier
  Glided to that better land.
When the flag went down the river
  Man and master both were free,
While the ringdove's note was mingled
  With the rippling Tennessee.

DIRGE FOR A SOLDIER.

IN MEMORY OF GEN. PHILIP KEARNY.

BY GEORGE H. BOKER.

CLOSE his eyes, his work is done!
What to him is friend or foeman,
Rise of moon, or set of sun,
Hand of man, or kiss of woman?
Lay him low, lay him low,
In the clover or the snow!
What cares he? he cannot know:
Lay him low!

As man may, he fought his fight,
Proved his truth by his endeavor;
Let him sleep in solemn night,
Sleep forever and forever.
Lay him low, lay him low,
In the clover or the snow!
What cares he? he cannot know:
Lay him low!

Fold him in his country's stars,
Roll the drum and fire the volley!
What to him are all our wars,

What but death bemocking folly?
Lay him low, lay him low,
In the clover or the snow!
What cares he? he cannot know:
Lay him low!

Leave him to God's watching eye,
Trust him to the hand that made him.
Mortal love weeps idly by:
God alone has power to aid him.
Lay him low, lay him low,
In the clover or the snow!
What cares he? he cannot know:
Lay him low!

THE CUMBERLAND.

ANONYMOUS.

MAGNIFICENT thy fate!
Once Mistress of the Seas,
No braver vessel ever flung
A pennon to the breeze;
No bark e'er died a death so grand;
Such heroes never vessel manned;
Your parting broadside broke the wave
That surged above your patriot grave;

Your flag, the gamest of the game,
  Sank proudly with you — not in shame,
But in its ancient glory ;
  The mem'ry of its parting gleam
Will never fade while poets dream ;
  The echo of your dying gun
Will last till man his race has run,
  Then live in angel story.

STARS IN MY COUNTRY'S SKY.

BY L. H. SIGOURNEY.

ARE ye all there ? Are ye all there,
  Stars of my country's sky ?
Are ye *all* there ? *Are ye all there,*
  In your shining homes on high ?
" Count us ! Count us," was their answer,
  As they dazzled on my view,
In glorious perihelion,
  Amid their field of blue.

I cannot count ye rightly ;
  There 's a cloud with sable rim ;
I cannot make your number out,
  For my eyes with tears are dim.

Oh! bright and blessed Angel,
  On white wing floating by,
Help me to count and not to miss
  One star in my country's sky!

Then the Angel touched mine eyelids,
  And touched the frowning cloud;
And its sable rim departed,
  And it fled with murky shroud.
There was no missing Pleiad,
  'Mid all that sister race;
The Southern Cross gleamed radiant forth,
  And the Pole star kept its place.

Then I knew it was the Angel
  Who woke the hymning strain
That at our dear Redeemer's birth
  Pealed out o'er Bethlehem's plain;
And still its heavenly key-tone
  My listening country held,
For all her constellated stars
  The diapason swelled.

Hartford, Conn.

OLD FANEUIL HALL.

BY EDWARD E. HALE.

COME soldiers, join a Yankee song,
And cheer us, as we march along,
With Yankee voices, — full and strong, —
Join in chorus all;
Our Yankee notions here we bring,
Our Yankee chorus here we sing, —
So make the Dixie forest ring
With "OLD FANEUIL HALL!"

When first our Fathers made us free,
When Old King George first taxed the tea,
They swore they would not bend the knee,
But armed them one and all!
In days like those the chosen spot
To keep the hissing water hot,
To pour the tea-leaves in the pot,
Was OLD FANEUIL HALL!

So when, to steal our tea and toast,
At Sumter first the Rebel host
Prepared to march along the coast,
At Jeff. Davis's call —

He stood on Sumter's tattered flag,
To cheer them with the game of brag;
He bade them fly his Rebel Rag
    On OLD FANEUIL HALL!

But war's a game that two can play;
They waked us up that very day,
And bade the Yankees come away
    Down South — at Abram's call!
And so I learned my facings right,
And so I packed my knapsack tight,
And then I spent the parting night
    In OLD FANEUIL HALL!

And on that day which draws so nigh
When rebel ranks our steel shall try, —
When sounds at last the closing cry
    "Charge bayonets — all!"
The Yankee shout from far and near,
Which broken ranks in flying hear,
Shall be a rousing Northern cheer
    From OLD FANEUIL HALL!

OUR UNION AND OUR FLAG.

BY RUTH N. CROMWELL.

MY flag, when first those starry folds
  Which waved o'er Sumter's band
Received the traitor's murderous fire,
  How flashed the tumult through the land.
No soul e'er panted for the hour
  That lifts it from love's torturing rack
As panted, then, a nation's heart
  To hurl the insult back.

If shame then hushed Columbia's breath
  And bowed her beauteous form,
'T was but the siroc's awful pause, —
  The lull before the storm.
Then men awoke, soul spoke to soul,
  And hand grasped hand, for woe or weal;
Then wavering hearts were turned to iron,
  And nerves were turned to steel.

Old feuds were not, old parties died;
  From vale to mountain crag,
A nation's shout linked friend and foe,
  Our Union and our flag;
We gave our men as freely then

As leaves from forest tree;
We gave our gold, as rivers give
Their waters to the sea.

Still floats on high Columbia's flag,
In the gloom of the autumn day, —
The blot still on her starry folds,
The stain not washed away;
Fort Moultrie stands, and Charleston lives,
And Freedom's sun grows pale;
Oh! God, whate'er thy children's doom,
Let not her foes prevail.

We point to Ellsworth's honored tomb,
To Lyon's fall, to Baker's grave;
What say Missouri's vine-clad hills?
What answer from Potomac's wave?
What answer they? Men ask of men
Who never yet foreswore the vow;
What answer they? the nation asks,
With lowering heart and brow.

Men, whom Columbia's voice hath call'd
To guide the ship of State,
Remember well each soul on board
Owns portion in her freight;
More clean was Nero's reeking brow,

More guiltless Arnold's past,
Than the hand that falters at the helm,
Or shrinks before the blast.

THE TWO FURROWS.

BY C. H. WEBB.

THE spring-time came — but not with mirth —
The banner of our trust,
And with it the best hopes of earth,
Were trailing in the dust.

The Farmer saw the shame from far,
And stopped his plough afield:
"Not the blade of peace but the brand of war
This arm of mine must wield.

"When traitor hands that flag would stain,
Their homes let women keep;
Until its stars burn bright again,
Let others sow and reap."

The Farmer sighed, — "A lifetime long
The plough has been my trust;
In truth it were an arrant wrong
To leave it now to rust."

With ready strength the Farmer tore
  The iron from the wood,
And to the village smith he bore
  That ploughshare stout and good.

The blacksmith's arms were bare and brown,
  And loud the bellows roared;
The Farmer flung his ploughshare down, —
  "Now forge me out a sword!"

And then a merry, merry chime
  The sounding anvil rung, —
Good sooth, it was a nobler rhyme
  Than ever poet sung.

The blacksmith wrought with skill that day,
  The blade was keen and bright;
And now where thickest is the fray
  The Farmer leads the fight.

Not as of old that blade he sways
  To break the meadow's sleep,
But through the rebel ranks he lays
  A furrow broad and deep.

The Farmer's face is burned and brown,
  But light is on his brow;

Right well he wots what blessings crown
The furrow of the Plough.

" But better is to-day's success," —
Thus ran the Farmer's word, —
" For nations yet unborn shall bless
This furrow of the Sword."

SHALL FREEDOM DROOP AND DIE?

BY CHARLES G. LELAND.

SHALL Freedom droop and die,
And we stand idle by,
When countless millions yet unborn
Will ask the reason why?

If for her flag on high
You bravely fight and die,
Be sure that God on his great roll
Will mark the reason why.

But should ye basely fly,
Scared by the battle-cry,
Then down through all eternity
You 'll hear the reason why.

THIS DAY, COUNTRYMEN.

BY ROBERT LOWELL.

COWARDS, slink away!
  But who scorns to see the foe
  Deal our land all shame and woe,
Must go forth, to-day!

Crops are safe, afield;
  Cripples and old men can reap;
  Young and strong and bold must leap
Other tools to wield.

Cast the daily trade!
  Never may be bought or won,
  After this great fight is done,
What, To-day, is weighed.

Leave your true-love's side!
  Go, be fearless and be strong:
  Woman glories to belong
Where she looks with pride.

True men hold our line:
  Basely leave their true ranks thin,

Waste and ruin will rush in,
Like the trampling swine.

Dare you be a man?
Now, for home and law and right,
Go, in God's name, to the fight!
Forward to the van!

MITCHEL.

BY W. FRANCIS WILLIAMS.

"*Hung be the Heavens with black.*"

HIS mighty life was burned away
By Carolina's fiery sun;
The pestilence that walks by day
Smote him before his course seemed run.

The constellations of the sky, —
The Pleiades, the Southern Cross, —
Looked sadly down to see him die,
To see a nation weep his loss.

"Send him to us," the stars might cry, —
You do not feel his worth below;

Your petty great men do not try
  The measure of his mind to know.

" Send him to us, — this is his place, —
  Not 'mid your puny jealousies ;
You sacrificed him in your race
  Of envies, strifes, and policies.

" His eye could pierce our vast expanse, —
  His ear could hear our morning songs, —
His mind, amid our mystic dance,
  Could follow all our myriad throngs.

" Send him to us ! No martyr's soul,
  No hero slain in righteous wars,
No raptured saint could e'er control
  A holier welcome from the stars."

Take him, ye stars ! Take him on high
  To your vast realms of boundless space ;
But once he turned from you to try
  His name on martial scrolls to trace.

That once was when his country's call
  Said danger to her flag was nigh ;
And then her banner's stars dimmed all
  The radiant lights which gemmed the sky.

Take him, loved orbs! His country's life, —
  Freedom for all, — for these he wars;
For these he welcomed bloody strife,
  And followed in the wake of Mars.

WHY?

BY RICHARD STORRS WILLIS.

TWENTY millions held at bay!
  Why, Northmen, why?
Less than half maintain the day!
  Why, Northmen, why?
With the sturdy iron will,
With the pluck, the dash, the skill,
With the blood of Bunker Hill, —
  Why, Northmen, why?

Standing yet are Sumter's walls, —
  Why, Northmen, why?
Slumbering yet th' avenging balls!
  Why, Northmen, why?
Charleston left to scoff at ease!
Richmond vaunting as it please!
Traitor-taunts on every breeze! —
  Why, Northmen, why?

Hear our wounded eagle wail!
  Why, Statesmen, why?
See our spangled banner trail!
  Why, Statesmen, why?
Coward England mocks amain!
Courtly Paris shrugs disdain!
Cordial Russia throbs with pain!—
  Why, Statesmen, why?

By this fierce, but fruitless fight,
  On! Leaders, on!
By your waste of loyal might,
  On! Leaders, on!
By the blood that soaks the sod,
By the Brave that bite the clod,
By the souls gone up to God!—
  On! Leaders, on!

By our Past, so bright-renown'd,
  On! Northmen, on!
By our Future, starry-crown'd!—
  On! Northmen, on!
By the South, deceived, misled,
By our Hundred Thousand Dead,
Who for South and North have bled!—
  On! Northmen, on!

December, 1862.

WHEN THE GREAT REBELLION 'S OVER.

ANONYMOUS.

CLIMBED the baby on her knee,
With an airy childish grace ;
Prattled in her lovely face, —
" When will papa come to me ? "
" Papa ? " soft the mother cried —
" Papa ! ah ! the naughty rover !
Sweet, my pet, he 'll come to thee
When the great Rebellion 's over ! "

" Mamma once had rosy cheeks,
Danced and sang a merry tune ;
Now she rocks me 'neath the moon,
Sits and sighs, but scarcely speaks."
Sad the smile the mother wore : —
" Sweet, mamma has lost her lover,
She will blush and sing no more
Till the great Rebellion 's over !

" Till the hush of peace shall come,
Like a quiet fall of snow,
And the merry troops shall go
Marching back to hearts at home."—
" Papá — home ? " the baby lisped,

Balmy breathed as summer clover;
  "Yes, my darling, home at last,
When the sad Rebellion 's over !"

Entered at the open door,
  While the mother soothed her child,
  One who neither spoke nor smiled,
Standing on the sunny floor.
  Wistful eyes met mournful eyes,
Hope took flight, like airy plover,
  Ah ! poor heart, thou 'lt wait in vain
Till the great Rebellion 's over !

Heart, poor heart ! too weak to save ;
  Vain your tears, — your longings vain, —
  Summer winds and summer rain
Beat already on his grave !
  From the flag upon his breast,
(Truer breast it ne'er shall cover !)
  From its mouldering colors, wet
  With his blood, shall spring beget
  Lily, rose, and violet,
And wreath of purple clover;
  With the flag upon his breast,
They have hid away your lover ; —
  Weep not, wail not ! let him rest,
  Having bravely stood the test,

He shall rank among the blest,
When the great Rebellion 's over!

A CHEER FOR THE BRAVE.

BY CAROLINE A. HOWARD.

LIFT up the starred banner, the pride of a nation,
Whose bulwarks are hearts firm and true as tried steel;
Bear the standard aloft with joyous elation,
The serpent is writhing 'neath Liberty's heel!

Blest ensign of Freedom, too long has thy glory
Been dimmed by the blight of disunion and shame;
Too long has rebellion, black-hearted and gory,
Ensanguined our land and dishonored our name!

Up Freedom! new courage! the struggle is closing!
Strike home for the right and forget not the brave,
Who, fighting and dying, forever repose in
The heart of their country, the soldier's true grave.

Be patient, yet rest not, nor fear the dark surges;
For our fathers of old were parted the seas;

Each wave of our progress the foeman submerges;
Then our cause give to God, and our Flag to the breeze.

June, 1862.

OUR COUNTRY'S CALL.

BY JOHN PIERPONT.

MEN who plough your granite peaks,
O'er whose head your Eagle shrieks,
And for aye of *Freedom* speaks,
Hear your country's call!
Swear, each loyal mother's son,
Swear " Our Country shall be ONE!"
Seize your sword, or bring your gun,
Bayonet and ball!

For the land that bore you — Arm!
Shield the State you love from harm!
Catch, and round you spread, the alarm;
Hear, and hold your breath!
Hark! the hostile horde is nigh!
See, the storm comes roaring by!
Hear and heed our battle-cry, —
" VICTORY OR DEATH!"

Sturdy landsmen, hearty tars,
Can you see your Stripes and Stars
Flouted by the three broad bars,
    And cold-blooded feel?
There the rebel banner floats!
Tyrants, vanquished by your votes,
Spring, like bloodhounds, at your throats:
    Let them bite your *steel!*

With no traitor at their head,
By no braggart coward led,
By no hero caught a-bed,
    While he dreamt of flight;
By no "Young Napoleons,"
Kept at bay by wooden guns,
Shall our brothers and our sons,
    Be held back from fight!

Like a whirlwind in its course,
Shall *again* a rebel force,
Jackson's foot or Stuart's horse,
    Pass our sleepy posts;
Roam, like Satan, "to and fro,"
And our Laggard let them go?
No! in thunder answer — "*No!*
    By the Lord of Hosts!"

With the Lord of Hosts we fight,
For his Freedom, Law, and Right, —
Strike for *these*, and his all-might
Shall with victory crown
Loyal brows, alive or dead;
Crush each crawling Copperhead,
And in bloody battle tread
This rebellion down!

Talk of "Peace," in hours like this?
'T is Iscariot's traitor kiss, —
'T is the Old Serpent's latest hiss!
Foil his foul intrigue!
Plant your heel his head upon!
Let him squirm! his race is run!
Now to *keep* your Country *one*,
Join our Union League!

THE OLD SHIP OF STATE.

BY DAVID BARKER, OF EXETER, ME.

O'ER the dark and gloomy horizon that bounds her,
Through the storm and the night and the hell that surrounds her,

I can see with a faith which Immortals have given,
Burning words, blazing out o'er the portals of
Heaven, —
"*She will live!*"

But a part of the freight which our forefathers
gave her
We must cast to the deep yawning waters to save
her:
'T is the *chain of the slave* we must fling out to light
her;
'T is the *brand* and the *whip* we must yield up to
right her.
She will live!

Clear the decks of the curse! If opposed by the
owner,
Hurl the wretch to the wave, as they hurled over
Jonah;
With a "Freedom to all!" gleaming forth from
our banner,
Let the tyrant yet learn we have freemen to man
her.
She will live!

She will live while a billow lies swelling before her,
She will live while the blue arch of heaven bends
o'er her,

While the name of a Christ to the fallen we cherish,
Till the hopes in the breast of humanity perish, —
She will live!

BATTLE-HYMN OF THE REPUBLIC.

BY MRS. JULIA WARD HOWE.

MINE eyes have seen the glory of the coming of the Lord;
He is trampling out the vintage where the grapes of wrath are stored;
He hath loosed the fateful lightning of His terrible swift sword:
His truth is marching on.

I have seen Him in the watchfires of a hundred circling camps;
They have builded Him an altar in the evening dews and damps;
I have read His righteous sentence by the dim and flaring lamps:
His day is marching on.

I have read a fiery gospel writ in burnished rows of steel:

" As ye deal with my contemners, so with you my
grace shall deal;
Let the Hero, born of woman, crush the serpent
with his heel,
Since God is marching on."

He has sounded forth the trumpet that shall never
call retreat;
He is sifting out the hearts of men before His judg-
ment-seat;
Oh! be swift, my soul, to answer Him! be jubilant,
my feet!
Our God is marching on.

In the beauty of the lilies Christ was born across
the sea,
With a glory in His bosom that transfigures you
and me;
As He died to make men holy, let us die to make
men free,
While God is marching on.

" OUT IN THE COLD."

WHAT is the threat? " Leave her out in the
cold!"

Loyal New England, too loyally bold:
Hater of treason, — ah! that is her crime!
Lover of Freedom, — too true for her time!

Out in the cold? Oh, she chooses the place,
Rather than share in a sheltered disgrace;
Rather than sit at a cannibal feast;
Rather than mate with the blood-reeking beast!

Leave out New England? And what will she do,
Stormy-browed sisters, forsaken by you?
Sit on her Rock, her desertion to weep?
Or, like a Sappho, plunge thence in the deep?

No; our New England can put on no airs, —
Nothing will change the calm look that she wears:
Life 's a rough lesson she learned from the first,
Up into wisdom through poverty nursed.

Not more distinct on his tables of stone
Was the grand writing to Moses made known,
Than is engraven, in letters of light,
On her foundations the One Law of Right.

She is a Christian: she smothers her ire,
Trims up the candle, and stirs the home fire;
Thinking and working and waiting the day
When her wild sisters shall leave their mad play.

Out in the cold, where the free winds are blowing;
Out in the cold, where the strong oaks are growing;
Guards she all growths that are living and great, —
Growths to rebuild every tottering State.

"Notions" worth heeding to shape she has wrought,
Lifted and fixed on the granite of thought:
What she has done may the wide world behold!
What she is doing, too, out in the cold!

Out in the cold! she is glad to be there,
Breathing the north wind, the clear healthful air;
Saved from the hurricane passions that rend
Hearts that once named her a sister and friend.

There she will stay, while they bluster and foam,
Planning their comfort when they shall come home;
Building the Union an adamant wall,
Freedom-cemented, that never can fall.

Freedom,—dear-bought with the blood of her sons,—
See the red current! right nobly it runs!
Life of her life is not too much to give
For the dear Nation she taught how to live.

Vainly they shout to you, sturdy Northwest!
'T is her own heart that beats warm in your breast;

Sisters in nature as well as in name;
Sisters in loyalty, true to that claim.

Freedom your breath is, O broad-shouldered North!
Turn from the subtle miasma gone forth
Out of the South land, from Slavery's fen,
Battening demons, but poisoning men!

Still on your Rock, my New England, sit sure,
Keeping the air for the great country pure!
There you the "wayward" ones yet shall enfold:
There they will come to you, out in the cold!

SONNET.

"THE VOICE WITHOUT AN ECHO."

BY C. K. TUCKERMAN.

When that distinguished defender of constitutional liberty, JOHN BRIGHT, M. P., of England, uttered his eloquent sentiments in behalf of the Federal Government, the "London Times" pronounced his address "a voice without an echo."

A VOICE went up in England, and was crowned
With dust and ashes. Baffled, blinded, lone,
It sunk upon the city's pavement-stone,
Where trampling Commerce all its utterance drowned.

Anon, by windy Prejudice 't was blown
Into the stately chambers of the throne —
For Parliamentary wisdom once renowned;
But there by red-taped Sophistry 't was bound, —
Bleeding and helpless, friendless and alone.
For England knew not what she yet shall own —
That where the wings of Justice once have flown,
They still shall fly, though beaten to the ground,
Bearing through Error's depths Truth's trumpet-tone,
Vital as light and boundless as the zone.

THE PRAYER OF A NATION.

BY WILLIAM H. BURLEIGH.

GOD of our fathers, hear our earnest cry!
Our hope, our strength, our refuge is with Thee!
Confound our foes and make their legions fly!
Strengthen our hosts and give them victory!
Victory — victory —
Oh, God of Armies! give us victory!

Not for exemption from the toil and loss,
The pains, the woes, the horrors of the strife,

But that with strong hearts we may bear the cross,
And welcome death to save our nation's life:
Victory — victory —
Oh, God of Battles! give us victory!

For this no costliest gift would we withhold;
For this we count not dear our loved repose,
Our teeming harvests, and our gathered gold,
Our commerce fanned by every wind that blows.
Victory — victory —
God of our fathers! give us victory!

Sons, brothers, sires, our bravest and our best, —
The dearest treasure love has sanctified, —
These have gone forth at Liberty's behest,
And on her altars have augustly died!
Victory — victory —
God of our martyrs! give us victory!

God! have they poured their priceless blood in vain?
Shall treason triumph in our nation's fall?
Shall Slavery weld once more her broken chain,
And o'er a prostrate land hold carnival?
Victory — victory —
Oh, God of Freedom! give us victory!

Nerve with new strength the patriot soldier's arm!
  Fill with new zeal the hero-souls that stand,
Pillars of fire, to save from deadliest harm
  Their children's birthright in this goodly land!
    Victory — victory —
  God of our heroes! give us victory!

For the sad millions of the groaning earth,
  Helpless and crushed beneath oppression's rod, —
For every hope that hallows home and hearth, —
  For heaven-born Liberty, the Child of God, —
    Victory — victory —
  God of the nations! give us victory!

From war's red hell, involved in smoke and flame,
  From up-piled altars of our noblest dead,
We cry to Thee! Oh, for Thy glorious name,
  Make bare Thine arm and smite our foes with dread!
    Victory — victory —
  Oh, God of Battles! give us victory!

THE WORD.

BY FORCEYTHE WILLSON.

ARM!
This is the trumpet-peal!
Arm!
Arm for the Commonweal!
Arm! Arm!

Arm!
Arm without any words!
Arm!
This is the time for swords!
Arm! Arm!

Arm to confront the foe
Arm!
Arm to return the blow!
Arm!

Arm ere it is too late!
Arm!
Arm or be desolate!
Arm!

Arm for your country and fly to defend her, —
Arm!

Arm now or never! Arm! or surrender!
Arm! Arm!

Arm for the Commonwealth, — Arm for your Mother, —
Your children, your firesides, and for each other!
Arm! Arm!

Arm for your Fatherhood!
Arm for your Motherhood!
Arm for your Sisterhood!
Arm for your Brotherhood!
Arm for Life, — Liberty, — and for all other good!
Arm! Arm!

Arm, Arm, to do and dare!
Arm for the Love you bear!
Arm for the Debonair!
Arm for the Heart that you live but to cherish!
Arm for the Free and Fair —
Arm for the Light and Air!
This is the last Appeal, — this your Country's cry, —
This is your mother's prayer!
— "Arm, My Beloved ones!
Arm, My Beloved Sons!
Arm, I implore you, and strike till you perish!"

THE PRESENT CRISIS.

BY JAMES RUSSELL LOWELL.

WHEN a deed is done for Freedom, through the broad earth's aching breast
Runs a thrill of joy prophetic, trembling on from East to West;
And the slave, where'er he cowers, feels the soul within him climb
To the awful verge of manhood, as the energy sublime
Of a century bursts full blossomed on the thorny stem of Time.

Through the walls of hut and palace shoots the instantaneous throe,
When the travail of the Ages wrings earth's systems to and fro;
At the birth of each new Era, with a recognizing start,
Nation wildly looks on nation, standing with mute lips apart,
And glad Truth's yet mightier man-child leaps beneath the Future's heart.

For mankind are one in spirit, and an instinct bears along,

Round the earth's electric circle, the swift flash of Right or Wrong;
Whether conscious or unconscious, yet humanity's vast frame,
Through its ocean-sundered fibres, feels the gush of joy or shame;
In the gain or loss of *one* race, *all the rest* have equal claim.

Once, to every man and nation, comes the moment to decide,
In the strife of Truth with Falsehood, for the good or evil side;
Some great cause, God's *new* Messiah, offering each the bloom or blight,
Parts the goats upon the left hand, and the sheep upon the right, —
And *the choice goes by forever* 'twixt that darkness and that light.

Hast thou chosen, O my people, in whose party thou shalt stand,
Ere the Doom from its worn sandals shakes the dust against our land?
Though the cause of Evil prosper, yet 't is Truth alone is strong;
And albeit she wander outcast now, I see around her throng

Troops of beautiful, tall angels, to enshield her
from all wrong.

We see dimly, in the Present, what is small and
what is great;
Slow of faith how weak an arm may turn the iron
helm of Fate;
But the soul is still oracular, — amid the market's
din,
List the ominous stern whisper from the Delphic
cave within:
"*They enslave their children's children, who make
compromise with Sin!*"

Slavery, the earth-born Cyclops, fellest of the giant
brood,
Sons of brutish Force and Darkness, who have
drenched the earth with blood,
Famished in his self-made desert, blinded by our
purer day,
Gropes in yet unblasted regions for his miserable
prey:
Shall we guide his gory fingers where our helpless
children play?

'T is as easy to be heroes, as to sit the idle slaves
Of a legendary virtue carved upon our fathers'
graves;

Worshippers of light *ancestral* make the *present*
light a crime.
Was the Mayflower launched by cowards? —
steered by men behind *their* time?
Turn those tracks toward Past, or *Future*, that
make Plymouth Rock sublime?

They were men of *present* valor, — stalwart old
iconoclasts;
Unconvinced by axe or gibbet that all virtue was
the Past's;
But we make *their* truth *our* falsehood, thinking
that has made *us* free,
Hoarding it in mouldy parchments, while our tender
spirits flee
The rude grasp of that great *Impulse* which drove
them across the sea.

New occasions teach new duties! Time makes
ancient good uncouth;
They must upward still, and onward, who would
keep abreast of Truth;
Lo, before us gleam her camp-fires! we *ourselves*
must Pilgrims be,
Launch *our* Mayflower, and steer boldly through
the desperate winter sea,
Nor attempt the Future's portal with the Past's
blood-rusted key.

ABRAHAM LINCOLN.

JANUARY FIRST, EIGHTEEN HUNDRED AND SIXTY-THREE.

BY W. D. GALLAGHER.

STAND like an anvil, when 't is beaten
 With the full vigor of the smith's right arm!
Stand like the noble oak-tree, when 't is eaten
 By the Saperda and his ravenous swarm!
For many smiths will strike the ringing blows
Ere the red drama now enacting close;
And human insects, gnawing at thy fame,
Conspire to bring thy honored head to shame.

Stand like the firmament, upholden
 By an invisible but Almighty hand!
He whomsoever JUSTICE doth embolden,
 Unshaken, unseduced, unawed shall stand.
Invisible support is mightier far,
With noble aims, than walls of granite are;
And simple consciousness of justice gives
Strength to a purpose while that purpose lives.

Stand like the rock that looks defiant
 Far o'er the surging seas that lash its form!
Composed, determined, watchful, self-reliant,
 Be master of thyself, and rule the storm!

And thou shalt soon behold the bow of peace
Span the broad heavens, and the wild tumult cease;
And see the billows, with the clouds that meet,
Subdued and calm, come crouching to thy feet.

Kentucky, December, 1862.

THE PROCLAMATION.

BY JOHN G. WHITTIER.

SAINT Patrick, slave to Milcho of the herds
Of Ballymena, sleeping, heard these words:
"Arise, and flee
Out from the land of bondage, and be free!"

Glad as a soul in pain, who hears from heaven
The angels singing of his sins forgiven,
And, wondering, sees
His prison opening to their golden keys,
He rose a Man who laid him down a Slave,
Shook from his locks the ashes of the grave,
And outward trod
Into the glorious liberty of God.

He cast the symbols of his shame away;
And passing where the sleeping Milcho lay,

Though back and limb
Smarted with wrong, he prayed, "God pardon
him!"

So went he forth: but in God's time he came
To light on Uilline's hills a holy flame;
And, dying, gave
The land a Saint that lost him as a Slave.

O, dark, sad millions, patiently and dumb
Waiting for God, your hour, at last, has come,
And Freedom's song
Breaks the long silence of your night of wrong!

Arise, and flee! shake off the vile restraint
Of ages! but, like Ballymena's saint,
The oppressor spare,
Heap only on his head the coals of prayer.

Go forth, like him! like him return again,
To bless the land whereon, in bitter pain,
Ye toiled at first,
And heal with Freedom what your Slavery cursed.

AN APPEAL.

BY OLIVER WENDELL HOLMES.

LISTEN, young heroes! your country is calling!
Time strikes the hour for the brave and the true!
Now, while the foremost are fighting and falling,
Fill up the ranks that have opened for you!

You whom the fathers made free and defended,
Stain not the scroll that emblazons their fame!
You whose fair heritage spotless descended,
Leave not your children a birthright of shame!

Stay not for questions while Freedom stands gasping!
Wait not till Honor lies wrapped in his pall!
Brief the lips' meeting be, swift the hands' clasping, —
"Off for the wars!" is enough for them all.

Break from the arms that would fondly caress you!
Hark! 'tis the bugle-blast, sabres are drawn!
Mothers shall pray for you, fathers shall bless you,
Maidens shall weep for you when you are gone!

Never or now! cries the blood of a nation,
  Poured on the turf where the red rose should
      bloom;
Now is the day and the hour of salvation, —
  Never or now! peals the trumpet of doom!

Never or now! roars the hoarse-throated cannon
  Through the black canopy blotting the skies;
Never or now! flaps the shell-blasted pennon
  O'er the deep ooze where the Cumberland lies!

From the foul dens where our brothers are dying,
  Aliens and foes in the land of their birth, —
From the rank swamps where our martyrs are lying
  Pleading in vain for a handful of earth, —

From the hot plains where they perish outnumbered,
  Furrowed and ridged by the battle-field's plough,
Comes the loud summons; too long you have slum-
      bered,
  Hear the last Angel-trump — Never or Now!

THE NEW REVEILLE.

BY WILLIAM O. BOURNE.

COME from the North, O freeman! Now or never!
Clothed in the panoply of right and power;
The foe is striving with a bold endeavor
To win the triumph in the noontide hour;
Come with the earnest of the blazing future!
Come with the burdens of the storied past!
Come with exultings in the mighty present,
And on the altar all your tribute cast.

Come from the pine-clad hills and furthest river,
That catch the rising of the eastern sun,
With sacred vows and giant will deliver
From treason's tread the land of WASHINGTON.
Come from the hills where fountains pure and gushing
Flow with the emblem of a better life;
Or, like the cataract in thunders rushing,
Press on and conquer in the holy strife.

Come from the loom where artist-hands are weaving
Their rare devices in the warp and woof;
The stronger web in Time's great loom is leaving
A mighty future to a tyrant's hoof;

With living threads that beat with love's pulsations,
And glow with images of Freedom's fire,
Weave now the destiny of coming nations,
That else shall gather at the solemn pyre!

Come from the fields, O brave and sturdy yeoman
Come from the hearthstones where ye love to sing!
Now is the hour to meet the bloody foeman,
Then back victorious all your laurels bring!
The songs of peace are for the day of triumph,
When Freedom's harvest all is gathered in.
Then come! on wider fields of truth and duty,
Reap long and well amid the battle din.

Come from the Keystone in the arch of Union!
Bring from the dark mines the treasures lying deep!
The fires grow hotter in the nation's furnace,
With fiercer blasts that will not let us sleep;
With stalwart arms our heroes now are moulding
Pillars of iron for our temple dome,
Which now we forge, while other lands, beholding,
Hear the great anvil ring in Freedom's home.

Come from the mountain, lake, and fertile prairie,
Blooming in verdure where the freemen toil;

Strike for the waters that shall onward carry
  Forth to the world the riches of your soil;
Strike for the freedom of the mighty river!
  Strike for the glory of your Western land!
Strike, freemen! till victorious blows shall shiver
  All the base foes that in your pathway stand.

Come from the South, O well-tried sons of sorrow!
  Come to the help of loyal men and true!
We fight and labor for the bright to-morrow,
  When vows of love the nation shall renew!
Come from the North! for so we sware forever!
  Come from the East, O sons of Pilgrim sires!
Come from the West, O brother! NOW OR NEVER!
  While Freedom kindles up immortal fires.

TO CANAÄN!

A SONG OF THE SIX HUNDRED THOUSAND.*

WHERE are you going, soldiers,
  With banner, gun, and sword?
We 're marching South to Canaän
  To battle for the Lord!

* See Numbers i. 45, 46.

What Captain leads your armies
  Along the rebel coasts?
The Mighty One of Israel,
  His name is Lord of Hosts!
      To Canaän, to Canaän
      The Lord has led us forth,
      To blow before the heathen walls
      The trumpets of the North!

What flag is this you carry
  Along the sea and shore?
The same our grandsires lifted up, —
  The same our father's bore!
In many a battle's tempest
  It shed the crimson rain, —
What God has woven in His loom
  Let no man rend in twain!
      To Canaän, to Canaän
      The Lord has led us forth,
      To plant upon the rebel towers
      The banners of the North!

What troop is this that follows,
  All armed with picks and spades?
These are the swarthy bondsmen, —
  The iron-skin brigades!
They'll pile up Freedom's breastwork,

They'll scoop out rebels' graves;
Who then will be their owner
And march them off for slaves?
To Canaän, to Canaän
The Lord has led us forth,
To strike upon the captive's chain
The hammers of the North!

What song is this you 're singing?
The same that Israel sung
When Moses led the mighty choir,
And Miriam's timbrel rung!
To Canaän! To Canaän!
The priests and maidens cried;
To Canaän! To Canaän!
The people's voice replied.
To Canaän, to Canaän
The Lord has led us forth,
To thunder through its adder dens
The anthems of the North!

When Canaän's hosts are scattered,
And all her walls lie flat,
What follows next in order?
— The Lord will see to that!
We 'll break the tyrant's sceptre, —
We 'll build the people's throne, —

When half the world is Freedom's
  Then all the world 's our own !
    To Canaän, to Canaän
    The Lord has led us forth,
    To sweep the rebel threshing-floors,
    A whirlwind from the North !

THE PATRIOT GIRL TO HER LOVER.

BY GEORGE VANDENHOFF.

HARK ! the trumpet is sounding, it 's a war-note I hear ;
  Arise, arm, and go forth my own Knight ;
And though my hand tremble, my eye drop a tear,
  I 'll gird on your sword for the fight !

O deem you the maid whose affection you claim,
  Though loving as I have loved you,
Could bear without blushing a recreant's name,
  To his country, to honor, untrue ?

You have vowed that your heart and your hopes are in *me*, —
  That you live in the light of my eyes ;
Let their lovebeam your beacon to victory be, —
  My hand of your valor the prize !

Would you win one? Be worthy of her who would die
Ere be link'd to a coward or slave;
And yielding her heart's blood would breathe but one sigh, —
A prayer her dear country to save.

Go forth then and conquer; be strong in the fight;
Think of me, and *put heart in each blow* .
Strike for Country, for UNION, for LOVE, and for RIGHT,
And down with the insolent foe!

WHO'S READY?

BY EDNA DEAN PROCTOR.

GOD help us! Who's ready? There's danger before!
Who's armed and who's mounted? The foe 's at the door!
The smoke of his cannon hangs black o'er the plain;
His shouts ring exultant while counting our slain;
And Northward and Northward he presses his line, —
Who's ready? O forward! — for yours and for mine!

No halting, no discord, the moments are Fates ;
To shame or to glory they open the gates !
There 's all we hold dearest to lose or to win ;
The web of the future to-day we must spin ;
And bid the hours follow with knell or with chime, —
Who 's ready ? O forward ! — while yet there is
time !

Lead armies or councils, — be soldier a-field, —
Alike, so your valor is Liberty's shield !
Alike, so you strike when the bugle-notes call,
For Country, for Fireside, for Freedom to All !
The blows of the boldest will carry the day, —
Who's ready ? O forward ! — there 's death in de-
lay !

Earth's noblest are praying, at home and o'er sea, —
" God keep the great nation united and free ! "
Her tyrants watch, eager to leap at our life,
If once we should falter or faint in the strife ;
Our trust is unshaken, though legions assail, —
Who 's ready ? O forward ! — and Right shall pre-
vail !

Who 's ready ? "*All* ready !" undaunted we cry ;
" For Country, for Freedom, we 'll fight till we die
No traitor, at midnight, shall pierce us in rest ;

No alien, at noonday, shall stab us abreast;
The God of our Fathers is guiding us still, —
All forward! we 're ready, and conquer we will!"

THE SNOW AT FREDERICKSBURG.

ANONYMOUS.

DRIFT over the slopes of the sunrise land,
  Oh wonderful, wonderful snow!
Oh! pure as the breast of a virgin saint,
  Drift tenderly, soft, and slow!
Over the slopes of the sunrise land,
  And into the haunted dells
Of the forests of pine, where the robbing winds
  Are tuning their memory bells.

Into the forests of sighing pines,
  And over those yellow slopes,
That seem but the work of the cleaving plough,
  That cover so many hopes!
They are many indeed, and straightly made,
  Not shapen with loving care;
But the souls let out and the broken blades
  May never be counted there!

Fall over those lonely hero graves,
  Oh delicate, dropping snow!
Like the blessing of God's unfaltering love
  On the warrior heads below!
Like the tender sigh of a mother's soul,
  As she waiteth and watcheth for One
Who will never come back from the sunrise land
  When this terrible war is done.

And here, where lieth the high of heart,
  Drift — white as the bridal veil
That will never be borne by the drooping girl
  Who sitteth afar, so pale.
Fall, fast as the tears of the suffering wife,
  Who stretcheth despairing hands
Out to the blood-rich battle-fields
  That crimson the Eastern sands.

Fall in thy virgin tenderness,
  Oh delicate snow, and cover
The graves of our heroes, sanctified, —
  Husband and son and lover!
Drift tenderly over those yellow slopes,
  And mellow our deep distress,
And put us in mind of the shriven souls
  And their mantles of righteousness!

BOSTON HYMN.

BY RALPH WALDO EMERSON.

THE word of the Lord by night
To the watching Pilgrims came,
As they sat by the sea-side,
And filled their hearts with flame.

God said, — I am tired of Kings,
I suffer them no more;
Up to my ear the morning brings
The outrage of the poor.

Think ye I made this ball
A field of havoc and war,
Where tyrants great and tyrants small
Might harry the weak and poor?

My angel, — his name is Freedom, —
Choose him to be your king;
He shall cut pathways east and west,
And fend you with his wing.

Lo! I uncover the land
Which I hid of old time in the West,
As the sculptor uncovers his statue,
When he has wrought his best.

I show Columbia, of the rocks
Which dip their foot in the seas,
And soar to the air-borne flocks
Of clouds, and the boreal fleece.

I will divide my goods;
Call in the wretch and slave:
None shall rule but the humble,
And none but toil shall have.

I will have never a noble,
No lineage counted great:
Fishers and choppers and ploughmen
Shall constitute a State.

Go, cut down trees in the forest,
And trim the straightest boughs;
Cut down trees in the forest,
And build me a wooden house.

Call the people together,
The young men and the sires,
The digger in the harvest-field,
Hireling and him that hires.

And here in a pine State-house
They shall choose men to rule

In every needful faculty, —
In church and state and school.

Lo, now! if these poor men
Can govern the land and sea,
And make just laws below the sun, —
As planets faithful be.

And ye shall succor men;
'T is nobleness to serve;
Help them who cannot help again;
Beware from right to swerve.

I break your bonds and masterships,
And I unchain the slave:
Free be his heart and hand henceforth,
As wind and wandering wave.

I cause from every creature
His proper good to flow:
So much as he is and doeth,
So much he shall bestow.

But, laying his hands on another
To coin his labor and sweat,
He goes in pawn to his victim
For eternal years in debt.

Pay ransom to the owner,
And fill the bag to the brim!
Who is the owner? The slave is owner,
And ever was. *Pay him!*

O North! give him beauty for rags,
And honor, O South! for his shame;
Nevada! coin thy golden crags
With Freedom's image and name.

Up! and the dusky race
That sat in darkness long, —
Be swift their feet as antelopes,
And as behemoth strong.

Come East and West and North,
By races, as snow-flakes,
And carry My purpose forth,
Which neither halts nor shakes.

My will fulfilled shall be,
For, in daylight or in dark,
My thunderbolt has eyes to see
His way home to the mark.

TO MY CHILDREN.

BY A SOLDIER IN THE ARMY.

DARLINGS — I am weary pining:
Shadows fall across my way;
I can hardly see the lining
Of the clouds — the silver lining,
Turning darkness into day.

I am weary of the sighing;
Moaning — wailing through the air;
Breaking hearts, in anguish crying
For the lost ones — for the dying,
Sobbing anguish of despair.

I am weary of the fighting:
Brothers, red with brother's gore.
Only, that the wrong we 're righting, —
Truth and Honor's battle fighting, —
I would draw my sword no more.

I am pining, dearest, pining,
For your kisses on my cheek;
For your dear arms round me twining;
For your soft eyes on me shining;
For your lov'd words; darlings — speak!

Tell me, in your earnest prattle,
  Of the olive branch and dove;
Call me from the cannon's rattle;
Take my thoughts away from battle;
  Fold me in your dearest love.

Darlings — I am weary pining:
  Shadows fall across my way;
I can hardly see the lining
Of the clouds — the silver lining,
  Turning darkness into day.

THE REFUGEE.

BY SAMUEL ECKEL, OF EAST TENNESSEE.

LONE upon the mountain summit,
  Watching through the weary night,
For the cheering heart-glow glimmer
  Of the Union camp-fire's light;

Starting at the slighest rustle
  In the leaves above my head;
Seeing foes in every shadow,
  While the morning light I dread;

In the distance, far below me,
  Tented foes I dimly trace;
The oppressors of my children,
  And the tyrants of my race.

I am black, — I sadly know it, —
  And for that I am a slave;
But I have a soul within me
  That will live beyond the grave.

Oft at noon, when I've been sitting
  'Neath some shady orange tree,
Every breeze would whisper to me
  That I must, I would be free.

Sadly I have mourned for freedom,
  But its breath I never drew;
Sadly mourn I for my children,
  They, alas! are chattels too.

Look! the morning dawns upon me;
  In the distant vale afar,
I behold a banner floating,
  I can see each stripe and star.

There I'll go and seek protection;
  And I ask, O God, of Thee,

That my cherished prayer be granted:
  Make oppressed bondmen free!

THE FIRST FIRE.

BY JOHN J. PIATT.

DEAREST, to-night upon our hearth
  See the first fire of Autumn leap, —
The first that we with festal mirth
  For loving Memory keep.
Sweet Fairy of the Fireside, come
And guard our altar-flame of Home!

Without, October breathes the night,
  Cold dews below, cold stars on high;
The chilly cricket sees our light
  Reach welcoming arms a-nigh,
And sighs to sing his evening song
Upon our hearth the winter long.

Blithe cricket! welcome, singing, here!
  I half recall dead Autumn's cold,
Half-close my eyes to dream, my dear,
  Their sadness vague and old:

The Fireside Fairy laughs and tries
With bursting sparks to shell my eyes!

Ill-timed the gay conceit, I know:
  On the dark hills that near us lie,
(The Real will not, need not go,)
  Beneath the Autumnal sky
Stand battle-tents that everywhere
Keep ghostly white the moonless air.

The sentinel walks his lonely beat,
  The soldier slumbers on the ground;
To one, hearth-glimmers far are sweet, —
  One dreams of fireside sound!
From unforgotten doors they reach,
Dear sympathies, more dear than speech.

I think of all the homeless woe,
  The battle-winter long;
Alas, the world —— the hearth 's a-glow!
  And lo, the cricket's song
Within! the Fairy's minstrel sings
Away the ghosts of saddest things!

The fire-smile keeps our walls in bloom; —
  Home's summer-light a flower, I deem;
And look, the pictures in the room,

How beautiful! a-gleam;
A window there with rose and bee, —
The Olive-Dove in from the sea!

A cottage in a summer land,
And one whose shadow walks before,
(Snow-peaks afar in sunset stand);
Vines flutter o'er the door,
Half-hiding in a sunlit place,
But cannot hide a sunlit face.

And, yonder, bending o'er a child,
An angel with a yearning grace,
Rosy with fire-bloom lingers mild, —
A mother's tender face!
Her wings (the boy has dreaming eyes)
Show that she came from Paradise.

Near by, the same; her arms about
A child just kissed from summer sleep
(Still rocks the cradle): laugh and shout
Within her bosom keep
Sweet echoes dancing. Which is best,
The angel, blessing — mortal blest?

A torrent lost in rainbow spray;
A flock (its shepherdess the moon)

Asleep; the laureate-lark of Day
  At home some even in June;
Dear humble fancies of the heart,
When Art was Love in love with Art!

Blithe dance the flames and blest are we!
  Without, the funeral of the year
Is preached by every mounful tree:
  The tree in blossom here
Knows no lost leaves, no farewell wing—
In vain will Autumn preach to Spring!

The cricket sings. Its song? You know,
  Warm prophecies of dearest days,—
(Horizons lost, of long ago,
  Crumble within the blaze!)
Of nights a-glow with light that blesses,
And wine from Home's enchanted presses.

The cricket sings, and, as I dream,
  Your face shows tender smile and tear,
What angels of the hearth a-gleam,
  Wingless, have lighted here?
Sing, cricket, sing of these to-night;
The first fire of our home is bright!

THE SOLDIER'S DEATH.

BY NANCY A. W. PRIEST.

THEY bore him to a cool and grassy place,
  So motionless they almost deemed him dead,
And fanned with tender care the pallid face,
  And with pure water bathed his drooping head,
Till his eyes opened, and a languid smile
  Played round his dying lips; and when he spoke,
They hushed their very breath to listen, while
  That low, faint murmur on the calm air broke.

"Comrades, my waning life is almost fled;
  Death's dampness gathers on my brow and cheek,
And from this gaping wound the bullet made,
  The crimson life-blood oozes while I speak.
I shall be resting quietly, ere long,
  And shall not need your love and tender care;
Your hearts are valiant and your arms are strong,
  Go back, my comrades, — you are needed there.

"But bear me first to yonder grassy sod,
  Whence I can turn my eyes upon the fight;
Gently — there. Leave me now alone with God,
  And go you back to battle for the right."

Then his mind wandered; and the beating drum,
The roar of cannon and the din of strife,
Changed to familiar, far-off sounds of home,
Or sweet, low tones of mother, child, or wife.

And the receding battle's frequent shocks,
Softened by distance, coming on the breeze,
Seemed to him like the bleating of the flocks,
Or hiveward murmur of the laden bees;
Until there came a mighty shout at length,
A cry that rose and swelled to "victory,"
And, opening his dim eyes with sudden strength,
He saw the foeman's ranks divide, and fly.

He rose, — he sat erect in his own blood;
His heart throbbed joyfully as when a boy;
"They fly, they fly!" he cried, and up to God
His spirit passed on that last shout of joy.
And so they found him when they sought him there,
Lifeless and cold in that secluded place, —
The rigid fingers clasped as if in prayer,
And that last smile of triumph on his face.

AFTER THE VICTORIES.

BY HOWARD GLYNDON.

HA! the wine-press of pain hath been trodden!
And suffering's meed mantles high, —
The perfect, rare wine, wrought of patience,
It moveth aright to the eye!
Oh! dark was the night while we trampled
Its death-purple grapes under foot;
And no song parted silence from darkness,
For Liberty's sibyl was mute!

And the fiends of the lowest were loosened,
To persecute Truth at their will!
They spat on her white shining forehead,
She standing unmoved and still!
The hiss of the white-blooded coward,
The vile breath of Calumny's brood,
Befouled and bedarkened the Kingdom,
And poisoned the place where we stood!

We — treading the ripe grapes asunder,
With failing and overworked feet;
Alone in the terrible darkness —
Alone in the stifling heat —
With agony-drops raining over

Our weak hands from desolate brows;
With a deadlier pain in our spirits,
O'er whose failure no promise arose!

Shook the innermost being of justice,
Stirred the innermost pulse of our God;
With a cry of remonstrance whose anguish
Frighted devils and saints from its road!
All the pain of a long-martyred nation,—
All its giant-heart's overtasked strength,—
In one Samson-like throe were unfettered,
Stànding up for a hearing at length!

And — even as we fell in the darkness —
Falling down, with our mouths in the dust;
With toil-stained and redly-dyed garments
That betokened us true to our trust,
When the laugh of the scoffer was loudest,
And the clapping of cowardly hands,
A glory blazed out from the Westward,
That startled the far distant lands!

. . . .

Ha! the wine-press of pain hath been trodden!
Now summon the laborers forth!
Let them come in their redly-dyed garments,
The lion-browed sons of the North!

Not for failure their veins have been leavened
  With the vintage of SEVENTY-SIX!
Nor unworthy the blood of our heroes
  With its rare olden currents to mix!

Ha! Conquerors! Come ye out boldly,
  Full fronting our reverent eyes!
In the might of your glorious manhood,
  Ye Saviours of Freedom, arise!
Come out in your sun-ripened grandeur,
  Ye victors, who wrestled with wrong!
Come! toil-worn and weary with battle —
  We greet you with shout and with song!

OUR UNION.

BY ALFRED B. STREET.

OUR Union, the gift of our fathers!
  In wrath roars the tempest above!
The darker and nearer our danger,
  The warmer and closer our love;
Though stricken, it never shall perish;
  It bends, but not breaks, to the blast;

Foes rush on in fury to rend it,
  But we will be true to the last.

Our Union, ordained by Jehovah, —
  Man sets not the fiat aside!
As well cleave the welkin asunder
  As the one mighty system divide.
The grand Mississippi sounds ever,
  From pine down to palm the decree;
The spindle, the corn, and the cotton, —
  One pean-shout, Union, to thee!

Our Union, the lightning of battle
  First kindled the flame of its shrine!
The blood and the tears of our people
  Have made it forever divine.
In battle we then will defend it!
  Will fight till the triumph is won!
Till the States form the realm of the Union
  As the sky forms the realm of the sun.

THE FISHERMAN OF BEAUFORT.

BY MRS. FRANCES D. GAGE.

THE tide comes up, and the tide goes down,
  And still the fisherman's boat,
At early dawn and at evening shade,
  Is ever and ever afloat:
His net goes down, and his net comes up,
  And we hear his song of glee :
"De fishes dey hates de ole slave nets,
  But comes to de nets of de free."

The tide comes up, and the tide goes down,
  And the oysterman below
Is picking away, in the slimy sands,
  In the sands ob de long ago.
But now if an empty hand he bears,
  He shudders no more with fear,
There 's no stretching board for the aching bones,
  And no lash of the overseer.

The tide comes up, and the tide goes down,
  And ever I hear a song,
As the moaning winds, through the moss-hung oaks,
  Sweep surging ever along :

"O massa white man! help de slave,
  And de wife and chillen too;
Eber dey 'll work, wid de hard, worn hand,
  Ef ell gib 'em de work to do."

The tide comes up, and the tide goes down,
  But it bides no tyrant's word,
As it chants unceasing the anthem grand
  Of its Freedom, to the Lord.
The fisherman floating on its breast
  Has caught up the key-note true:
"De sea works, massa, for 't sef and God,
  And so must de brack man too.

"Den gib him* de work, and gib him de pay,
  For de chillen and wife him love;
And de yam shall grow, and de cotton shall blow,
  And him nebber, nebber rove;
For him love de ole Carlina State,
  And de ole magnolia-tree:
Oh! nebber him trouble de icy Norf,
  Ef de brack folks am go free."

* The colored people use the word "him" for "us," and apply the same pronoun to animate and inanimate objects, whether of masculine, feminine, or neuter gender.

UNITED STATES NATIONAL ANTHEM.

DEDICATED TO SAMUEL C. REED, ESQ.

BY WILLIAM ROSS WALLACE.

GOD of the Free! upon Thy breath
  Our Flag is for the Right unrolled,
As broad and brave as when its Stars
  First lit the hallowed time of old.

For Duty still its folds shall fly;
  For Honor still its glories burn,
Where Truth, Religion, Valor, guard
  The patriot's sword and martyr's urn.

No tyrant's impious step is ours;
  No lust of power on nations rolled:
Our Flag — for *friends*, a starry sky;
  For *traitors*, storm in every fold.

O thus we 'll keep our Nation's life,
  Nor fear the bolt by despots hurled;
The blood of all the world is here,
  And they who strike us strike the world!

God of the Free! our Nation bless
  In its strong manhood as its birth;

And make its life a Star of Hope
  For all the struggling of the Earth.

Then shout beside thine Oak, O North!
  O South! wave answer with thy Palm;
And in our Union's heritage
  Together sing the Nation's Psalm!

ODE.

BY HENRY T. TUCKERMAN.*

FROM youth's dear haunts resounding
  What hallowed voices call;
Her shrine once more surrounding
  With love that welcomes all!
By life's stern tasks undaunted,
  With memory's light imbued,
Here where truth's seeds were planted
  Her blossoms are renewed.

Ere savage foes were banished,
  Began Art's peaceful rule;

* At the Centennial Celebration of Dummer Academy, Newbury, Mass., (1863,) this Ode, — written for the occasion by H. T. Tuckerman, a former pupil, — was sung to the tune of the Missionary Hymn.

Ere ancient woods had vanished,
  Here rose the church and school;
And to their bounteous mother
  The children now repair,
Each fond and faithful brother, —
  With festal song and prayer.

Though battle-clouds may lower
  Around our harvest-day,
And treason's subtle power
  The patriot's hope delay;
Though error's blighting traces
  And sorrow's pensive shade
May calm exultant faces,
  And pleasure's dream upbraid;

Divine the hand whose guiding
  Has brought us safely back, —
Benign the strife whose chiding
  Has taught us duty's track;
And blest the faith and learning,
  New England, true and brave,
As altar lamps keep burning,
  Our freedom's ark to save!

HO! SONS OF THE PURITAN.

The Cavaliers, Jacobites, and Huguenots who settled the South, naturally hate, condemn and despise the Puritans who settled the North. The former are master races; the latter, a slave race, descendants of the Saxon serfs. [*De Bow's Review.*

——— who through a cloud,
Not of war only but detractions rude,
Guided by faith and matchless fortitude,
To peace and truth thy glorious way hast ploughed,
Milton's Sonnet to Cromwell.

HO! sons of the Puritan! sons of the Roundhead,
Leave your fields fallow and fly to the war;
The foe is advancing, the trumpet hath sounded,—
To the rescue of freedom, truth, justice, and law!
Hear His voice bid ye on
Who spake unto Gideon:
"Rend the curtains of Midian
From Heshbon to Dor!"

From green-covered Chalgrave, from Naseby and Marston,
Rich with the blood of the Earnest and True,
The war-cry of Freedom, resounding hath passed on
The wings of two centuries, and come down to you:

"Forward! to glory ye,
Though the road gory be!
Strong of arm — let your story be —
And swift to pursue!"

List! list! to the time-honored voices that loudly
Speak from our Mother-land o'er the sad waves,—
From Hampden's dead lips, and from Cromwell's, who proudly
Called freemen to palaces, — tyrants to graves:
"Sons of the Good and Pure!
Let not their blood endure
The attaint of a brood impure
Of cowards and slaves!"

And old Massachusetts' hills echo the burden:
"Sons of the Pure-in-heart never give o'er!
Though blood flow in rivers, and death be the guerdon,
All the sharper your swords be,— death welcome the more!
Swear yé to sheathe your swords
Not till the heathen hordes
On their craven knees breathe the words,
'*The Lord's we restore!*'"

Accursed be the land that shall give ye cold greeting, —

Cursed in its coffers, and cursed in its fame!
And woe to the traitors, feigning friendship, and meeting
Your trust with assassins' dark weapons of shame!
As did Penuel's high
Parapets lowly lie,
And the princes of Succoth die,
So fare these the same!

Though sharp be the throes of these last tribulations,
Look ye! a brighter dawn kindles the day!
O, children of Saints, and the hope of the Nation,
Look aloft! your deliverance cometh for aye!
Soon, from those fairer skies,
White-winged, the herald flies
To the warders of Paradise,
To call them away!

Then on to the battle-shock! and if in anguish,
Gasping, and feeble-pulsed, low on the field,
Struck down by the traitor's fell prowess ye languish,
In Jehovah behold ye your Refuge and Shield!
Or, if in victory,
Doubts shall come thick to ye,
Trust in Him — He shall speak to ye
The mystery revealed.

Ho! sons of the Puritan! sons of the Roundhead
  Leave your fields fallow, your ships at the shore!
The foe is advancing — the trumpet hath sounded,
  And the jaws of their Moloch are dripping with gore!
    Raise the old pennon's staff!
    Let the fierce cannon's laugh,
    Till the votaries of Ammon's calf
    Blaspheme ye no more!

A PLAINT FROM SAVAGE'S.

BY GEORGE ALFRED TOWNSEND.

I.

ALAS! for the pleasant peace we knew
  In the happy summers of long ago,
When the rivers were bright and the skies were blue
  By the homes of Henrico.
We dreamed of wars that were far away,
  And read, as in fable, of blood that ran
Where the James and Chickahominy stray,
  Through the groves of Powhattan.

II.

'T is a dream come true, for the afternoons
  Blow bugles of war by our fields of grain,
And the sabres sink as the dark dragoons
  Come galloping up the lane;
The pigeons have flown from the eaves and tiles,
  The oat-blades have grown to blades of steel,
And the Huns swarm down the leafy aisles
  Of the grand old Commonweal.

III.

They have torn the Indian fisher's nets
  Where the gray Pamunkey goes toward the sea,
And blood runs red in the rivulets
  That babbled and brawled in glee;
The corpses are strewn in Fairy Oak glades,
  The hoarse guns thunder from Drury's Ridge,
The fishes that played in the cool deep shades
  Are frightened from Bottom Bridge.

IV.

I would that the year were blotted away,
  And the strawberries green in the hedge again;
That the scythe might swing in the tangled hay,
  And the squirrels romp in the glen;
The walnuts sprinkle the clover slopes
  Where graze the sheep and the spotted steer,

And the winter restore the golden hopes
  That were trampled in a year.

Michie's Farm, Savage's Station, Va.

THE VARUNA.

SUNK APRIL TWENTY-FIFTH, 1862.

BY GEORGE H. BOKER.

WHO has not heard of the dauntless Varuna?
  Who has not heard of the deeds she has done?
Who shall not hear, while the brown Mississippi
  Rushes along from the snow to the sun?

Crippled and leaking she entered the battle,
  Sinking and burning she fought through the fray,
Crushed were her sides and the waves ran across her,
  Ere, like a death-wounded lion at bay,
Sternly she closed in the last fatal grapple,
  Then in her triumph moved grandly away.

Five of the rebels, like satellites, round her,
  Burned in her orbit of splendor and fear:
One, like the pleiad of mystical story,
  Shot, terror-stricken, beyond her dread sphere.

We who are waiting with crowns for the victors,
Though we should offer the wealth of our store,
Load the Varuna from deck down to kelson,
Still would be niggard, such tribute to pour
On courage so boundless. It beggars possession,
It knocks for just payment at heaven's bright door!

Cherish the heroes who fought the Varuna;
Treat them as kings if they honor your way;
Succor and comfort the sick and the wounded;
Oh! for the dead, let us all kneel to pray.

THE BATTLE AUTUMN OF 1862.

BY JOHN G. WHITTIER.

THE flags of war like storm-birds fly,
The charging trumpets blow;
Yet rolls no thunder in the sky,
No earthquake strives below.

And calm and patient nature keeps
Her ancient promise well,
Though o'er her bloom and greenness sweeps
The battle's breath of hell.

And still she walks in golden hours
  Through harvest-happy farms,
And still she wears her fruits and flowers
  Like jewels on her arms.

What means the gladness of the plain,
  This joy of eve and morn,
The mirth that shakes the beard of grain,
  And yellow locks of corn?

Ah! eyes may well be full of tears,
  And hearts with hate are hot;
But even paced come round the years,
  And Nature changes no.

She meets with smiles our bitter grief,
  With songs our groans of pain;
She mocks with tint of flower and leaf
  The war-field's crimson stain.

Still in the cannon's pause we hear
  Her sweet thanksgiving psalm;
Too near to God for doubt or fear,
  She shares the eternal calm.

She knows the seed lies safe below
  The fires that blast and burn;

For all the tears of blood we sow,
  She waits the rich return.

She sees, with clearer eye than ours,
  The good of suffering born, —
The hearts that blossom like her flowers,
  And ripen like her corn.

Oh! give to us, in times like these,
  The vision of her eyes;
And make her eyes and fruited trees
  Our golden prophecies!

Oh! give to us her finer ear!
  Above this stormy din;
We too would hear the bells of cheer
  Ring peace and freedom in.

OUR COUNTRY.

YE sailors on the mighty deep,
  Ye soldiers of the land,
Your sacred oaths we bid ye keep,
  We bid ye faithful stand.
This broad land, this whole land, this free land is yours, —
It is the noble Union your Constancy secures!

No narrow State in this dread hour
  Shall dare to claim your birth,
Allegiance to the Federal power
  Is more than Home or Hearth.
This broad land, this whole land, this free land is yours, —
It is the noble Union your Loyalty secures!

Keep ye the mighty river
  Unbroken in its tide,
And the hills that stand forever,
  Let no mean hand divide.
This broad land, this whole land, this free land is yours, —
It is the noble Union your Fidelity secures!

The laws your fathers writ in blood
  No impious thought shall break,
The flag they bore through fire and flood
  Let no true heart forsake.
This broad land, this whole land, this free land is yours, —
It is the noble Union your Bravery secures!

SYMPATHY.

BY MRS. L. H. SIGOURNEY.

MY country weepeth sore
  Above her fallen brave,
By field, by grove, by stream they lie,
Their faces toward their native sky,
  And scarcely find a grave.

She listeneth to the wail
  That from a thousand homes
By town, by tower, by prairie bright,
At dawn, at noon, at dead of night,
  In wild discordance comes.

She at the threshold grieves,
  Where stretched on pallets lie,
Beneath the surgeon's scalpel keen,
The stalwart form, the noble mien,
  Convulsed with agony.

She bendeth o'er the wave,
  Where sank the patriot train
Whose volleying guns a farewell sent,
As downward with their ship they went,
  To the unfathomed main.

She listeneth as the Earth,
  Surcharg'd with bloody rain,
Her many cherished sons demands:
Her bold, her beautiful, whose hands
  Made rich her harvest-wain.

She kneeleth at the Throne
  Of mercy, day and night;
She looketh o'er the war-cloud dim,
With an unwavering trust in Him
  Who doeth all things right.

CLARIBEL'S PRAYERS.

THE day, with cold, gray feet, clung shivering to the hills,
  While o'er the valley, still night's rain-fringed curtains fell;
But waking blue eyes smiled. "'T is ever as God wills;
  He knoweth best, and be it rain or shine, 't is well,
    Praise God!" cried always little Claribel.

Then sank she on her knees. With eager, lifted hands,

Her rosy lips made haste some dear request to tell:
"O Father! smile, and save this fairest of all lands,
And make her free, whatever hearts rebel.
Amen! Praise God!" cried little Claribel.

"And, Father," still arose another pleading prayer,
"Oh! save my brother, in the rain of shot and shell;
Let not the death-bolt, with its horrid streaming hair,
Dash light from those sweet eyes I love so well.
Amen! Praise God!" wept little Claribel.

"But, Father, grant that when the glorious fight is done,
And up the crimson sky the shouts of Freedom swell,
Grant that there be no nobler victor 'neath the sun
Than he whose golden hair I love so well.
Amen! Praise God!" cried little Claribel.

When gray and dreary day shook hands with grayer night,
The heavy air was filled with clangor of a bell.
"Oh, shout!" the herald cried, his worn eyes brimmed with light:

"'T is victory! Oh! what glorious news to tell!"
"Praise God! He heard my prayer," cried Claribel.

"But, pray you, soldier, was my brother in the fight,
And in the fiery rain? Oh! fought he brave and well?"
"Dear child," the herald cried, "there was no braver sight
Than his young form, so grand 'mid shot and shell."
"Praise God!" cried trembling little Claribel.

"And rides he now with victor's plumes of red,
While trumpets' golden throats his coming steps foretell?"
The herald dropped a tear: "Dear child," he softly said,
"Thy brother evermore with conquerors shall dwell."
"Praise God! He heard my prayer," cried Claribel.

"With victors wearing crowns and bearing palms," he said;

And snow of sudden fear upon the rose-lips fell.
"Oh! sweetest herald, say my brother lives," she plead.
"Dear child, he walks with angels who in strength excel.
Praise God, who gave this glory, Claribel."

The cold, gray day died sobbing on the weary hills,
While bitter mourning on the night-wind rose and fell.
"Oh, child," the herald wept, "'t is as the dear Lord wills,
He knoweth best; and be it life or death, 't is well."
"Amen! Praise God!" sobbed little Claribel.

CHRISTMAS AND NEW YEAR, 1862–3.

BY LUCY LARCOM.

OUR Christmas dawns on bloody times;
The battle-clarion wakes the blast;
The funeral-drums throb thick and fast,
And drown the merry morning-chimes.

Yet keep, O land, your festival,
  In memory of the Man who came, —
  The Man Divine, to bear our blame,
And breathe His blessings over all!

He reigns not yet the Prince of Peace:
  He came to bring on earth a sword.
  Till men love Freedom's Gospel word,
The sound of war shall never cease.

'T was Liberty he came to bring.
  When He ascended up on high,
  He captive led captivity,
And made the world with Freedom ring.

This glorious gift He gave to men.
  The stronger from the weaker steals;
  But hark! a clang of triumph peals!
The lost shall be restored again.

Behold, O army of the Lord;
  The presence that among you stands!
  Most clean, most pure, must be the hands
That close on victory His award.

O nation working His behest;
  O army raised to wage His war,

Accept the end He called you for,
And soon the land shall be at rest.

Give freely as of old He gave;
Your fathers owned the boon from Him.
Before the golden hour grows dim,
Stamp it with FREEDOM for the slave.

Ye hear, ye children of the free;
And where an ancient wrong hath stood,
Ye plant, and water with your blood,
Your Christmas Tree of Liberty.

The Christ-Child smiles its branches through,
With heaven's clear smile on black and white;
The Tree has filled the land with light
And cooled its wounds with balm and dew.

Dark faces, you no more shall be
Darker with shadows of our hate;
Receive our greeting-gift, though late,
A Happy New-Year, and be Free!

THE COLOR SERGEANT.

BY A. D. F. RANDOLPH.

YOU say that in every battle
  No soldier was braver than he,
As, aloft in the roar and the rattle,
  He carried the flag of the Free:
I knew, ah! I knew he 'd ne'er falter,
  I could trust him, the dutiful boy.
My Robert was wilful, — but Walter,
  Dear Walter, was ever a joy.

And if he was true to his mother,
  Do you think he his trust would betray,
And give up his place to another,
  Or turn from the danger away?
He knew while afar he was straying,
  He felt in the thick of the fight,
That at home his poor mother was praying
  For him and the cause of the Right!

Tell me, comrade, who saw him when dying,
  What he said, what he did, if you can;
On the field in his agony lying,
  Did he suffer and die like a man?
Do you think he once wished he had never

Borne arms for the Right and the True?
Nay, he shouted Our Country forever!
When he died he was praying for you!

O my darling! my youngest and fairest,
Whom I gathered so close to my breast;
I called thee my dearest and rarest,
And thou wert my purest and best!
I tell you, O friend! as a mother,
Whose full heart is breaking to-day,
The Infinite Father — none other —
Can know what He's taken away.

I thank you once more for your kindness,
For this lock of his auburn hair:
Perhaps 't is the one I in blindness
Last touched, as we parted just there!
When he asked, through his tears, should he linger
From duty, I answered him, Nay:
And he smiled, as he placed on my finger
The ring I am wearing to-day.

I watched him leap into that meadow;
There, a child, he with others had played;
I saw him pass slowly the shadow
Of the trees where his father was laid;
And there, where the road meets two others,

Without turning, he went on his way:
Once his face toward the foe — not his mother's
Should unman him, or cause him delay.

It may be that some day your duty
Will carry you that way again;
When the field shall be riper in beauty,
Enriched by the blood of the slain;
Would you see if the grasses are growing
On the grave of my boy? Will you see
If a flower, e'en the smallest, is blowing,
And pluck it, and send it to me?

Don't think, in my grief, I'm complaining;
I gave him, God took him, 't is right;
And the cry of his mother remaining
Shall strengthen his comrades in fight.
Not for vengeance, to-day, in my weeping,
Goes my prayer to the Infinite Throne.
God pity the foe when he's reaping
The harvest of that he has sown!

Tell his comrades these words of his mother:
All over the wide land to-day,
The Rachels, who weep with each other,
Together in agony pray.
They know, in their great tribulation,

By the blood of their children outpoured,
We shall smite down the foes of the Nation,
In the terrible day of the Lord.

MASSACHUSETTS.

BY B. P. SHILLABER.

I HEAR an army's mighty tread,
  And the sound of war's alarms;
I read a thought, serene but dread,
  Written in gleaming arms;
A solemn *purpose* fills the air
Like the holy effluence of prayer.

I feel the thrill of a people's heart
  In the drum-tap's stirring beat,
And the quickened pulse's fervid start
  In the rush of hasty feet,
And the gleam of vengeful glances shines
Along the bayonets' glistening lines.

I see a nation's triumph stand
  In acts of generous trust,
Where wealth unclasps its iron hand

And scatters the needed dust, —
Giving the sinews of golden life
To the holy cause of Freedom's strife.

'T is Massachusetts' glance of light, —
The glare of the glittering steel,—
The earnest of her awful might
In the vital thrill we feel;
And her voice is the cannon's blasting breath
That speaks to Treason the doom of Death.

Honest old Commonwealth! to thee
Thy children look with pride:
Thy name 's a password to the Free,
With Right identified;
Thy bidding we hear, like a mother's word,
And our hearts to their deepest depths are stirred.

God bless thee! every heart outpours,
And every arm grows strong,
From mountain bound to ocean shores,
Thy glory to prolong;
To live in thy cause is an honor high
But a greater in such a cause to die.

THE SOLDIER'S SWEETHEART.

BY GEORGE W. BUNGAY.

I GO down to the sea,
Where the waves speak to me
Of my darling, the soul of my soul;
But her footprints no more
Mark the desolate shore,
Where she tempted the billows to roll.

There the sad billows break,
Like my heart for her sake,
On the lonely and desolate shore;
For the waves of the sea
Are now sighing with me,
For a mortal, now mortal no more.

With my heart filled with tears,
And my hopes chilled with fears,
By the grave of my darling I knelt;
And I uttered a prayer
On the listening air,
Whose dew wept the sorrow I felt.

There the winds wove a shroud
Of a dim passing cloud,

Betwixt me and the bright stars above;
    And the form in its fold,
    Like the shape under mould,
Was the form of the angel I love.

    Would that I were a flower,
    Born of sunshine and shower;
I would grow on the grave of the dead.
    I would sweeten the air
    With the perfume of prayer,
Till my soul on its incense had fled.

    And I never would fade
    In the delicate shade
Of the tree in whose shadow she lies.
    There my petals should bloom,
    By her white rural tomb,
When the stars closed their beautiful eyes.

    Now I see her in dreams
    On the banks of the streams,
In the dear land of exquisite bliss,
    Where the sweep of her wings,
    And the song that she sings,
Oft awake me to sadness in this.

THE RISING OF THE NORTH.

HIGH on the mountains
  A new day is dawning;
Over the eastern hills
  Breaks the glad morning.

Up from the valleys
  Glad eyes are turning,
Full of the holy fires
  In the heart burning.

Long was the night-watch,
  Bitter with woe;
Dim burned the altar-fires, —
  Faintly and low.

Now, from the orient,
  Leaps the new day,
Chasing the shadows
  Of midnight away.

Freedom has risen,
  And men shall once more
Gird on the armor
  Their forefathers wore.

And dare to do battle
For Justice and Right;
Die as their fathers died, —
Facing the fight.

Like some old organ-peal,
Solemn and grand,
The anthem of Freedom
Sweeps through the land.

The hand of a master
Touches the keys,
And the soul-stirring symphony
Swells on the breeze.

Out of the clouded sky
A new light is breaking;
From the deep sleep of guilt
The nation is waking.

High on the mountains
The new day is dawning;
Soon in the valleys
Shall break the glad morning.

Cambridge, Mass. J. N. M.

THE CAVALRY CHARGE.

BY EDMUND C. STEDMAN.

OUR good steeds snuff the evening air,
  Our pulses with their purpose tingle;
The foeman's fires are twinkling there
  He leaps to hear our sabres jingle!
          HALT!
  Each carbine sent its whizzing ball:
  Now, cling! clang! forward all,
          Into the fight!

Dash on beneath the smoking dome:
  Through level lightnings gallop nearer!
One look to Heaven! No thoughts of home:
  The guidons that we bear are dearer.
          CHARGE!
  Cling! clang! forward all!
  Heaven help those whose horses fall:
          Cut left and right!

They flee before our fierce attack!
  They fall! they spread in broken surges.
Now, comrades, bear our wounded back,
  And leave the foeman to his dirges.
          WHEEL!

The bugles sound the swift recall:
Cling! clang! backward all!
Home, and good-night!

THE WIDOWED SWORD.

ANONYMOUS.

THEY have sent me the sword that my brave boy wore
On the field of his young renown, —
On the last red field, where his faith was sealed,
And the sun of his days went down.
Away with the tears
That are blinding me so;
There is joy in his years,
Though his young head be low;
And I'll gaze with a solemn delight, evermore,
On the sword that my brave boy wore.

'T was for Freedom and Home that I gave him away,
Like the sons of his race of old;
And though, aged and gray, I am childless this day,
He is dearer a thousandfold.
There 's a glory above him

To hallow his name;
A land that will love him
Who died for its fame;
And a solace will shine when my old heart is sore,
Round the sword that my brave boy wore.

All so noble, so true, — how they stood, how they fell
In the battle, the plague, and the cold;
Oh, as bravely and well as e'er story could tell
Of the flower of the heroes of old.
Like a sword through the foe
Was that fearful attack,
That so bright ere the blow
Comes so bloodily back;
And foremost among them, his colors he bore, —
And here is the sword that my brave boy wore.

It was kind of his comrades, ye know not how kind;
It is more than the Indies to me;
Ye know not how kind and how steadfast of mind
The soldier to sorrow can be.
They know well how lonely,
How grievously wrung,
Is the heart that its only
Love loses so young;

And they closed his dark eyes when the battle was o'er,
And sent his old father the sword that he wore.

THE CHANT OF TREASON.

BY HENRY BERGH.

WHEN suspicion is lulled, when confidence reigns,
When daylight departs, and darkness attains;
When innocence sleeps, and honor reposes,
When industry rests on its pillow of roses;
When the justice of man is drugg'd with deceit,
And the plans of the traitor are all complete!
Then — goblet on high,
Hark! to his mad cry:
Hurrah! here's success to bold Treason!

What though that ancient and world-honored State,
Whose laws both protect the small and the great,
That freights every ambient breath of the sea
With tidings of Hope to the Slave — from the Free?
What though its banner be spangled with stars,

Was woven 'mid blood, privations, and scars?
Well! what 's that to me?
Come, join in the glee:
Hurrah! here 's success to bold Treason!

In every age, and in every clime,
I 've lived, and shall live, to the end of Time!
No country have I, no watchword I cry,
I dwell in the soul, I speak through the eye;
In earth — in the air — in the bubbling stream —
I lurk unsuspected — my sway is supreme!
So, fill up the glass,
And let the toast pass:
Hurrah! here 's success to bold Treason!

In places of trust, in the Forum I sit;
In the Council of State my meshes I knit:
By the side of the nation's honored choice
Is heard my subdued, pestiferous voice;
And the sinews of war — the army and fleet —
Are toys for my genius to work out defeat:
So, drink of the bowl,
Without stint or toll:
Hurrah! here 's success to bold Treason!

Would'st learn whence I came, — the name of my sire?

I 'm issue of Hell, I 'm Destruction — dire !
On man's perjured faith, and war's cruel blast;
On the groans of the slave, I make my repast;
In paralyzed trade, — in commerce destroyed, —
In national ruin, — my means are employed.
Then drink, drink, my friends,
The toast Treason sends:
Hurrah ! here 's success to bold Treason !

But, lo ! in ocean's indistinct distance,
What ensigns are those in hostile resistance ?
How, like a monster in pained respiration,
The sea bears them down, concealing their nation.
Now they rise : one is ours — " the skull and cross bars ; "
The other is Freedom's ! the proud Stripes and Stars !
Bang ! bang ! hear the roar !
It sinks — it is o'er !
Hurrah ! here 's success to bold Treason !

And yet there are times, I frankly declare,
When these triumphs much more resemble despair;
And that flag which we saw just now in the skies,
With memories haunt me — o'erflowing my eyes;
And could I return — nay, heed not, I pray,
I wander in mind, knowing not what I say.

Shout! shout! I implore,
Louder still than before:
Hurrah! here 's success to bold Treason!

Again yonder flag! sank it not 'neath the main?
Behold, it is up — high as ever again!
What means that acclaim? the plank, spar, and rope!
Great God, they 're for me! 't is the death-knell of hope!
Adieu, friends — I choke — I strangle — I die!
Hark, hark! to that deaf'ning, triumphant cry; —
Fill, fill to the brim,
Chant Columbia's hymn!
Hurrah! here is *death* to bold Treason!

London American, March, 1861.

THE FALLEN SOLDIER.

BEAR off your comrade, boys! See, he has fallen;
The blow at his leader aimed, he made his own:
Loose from the bridle the stiffened hand, softly:
Only this morning it fed his good roan.

Who knows this brave lad, for he scarce can be
twenty,
That just for his country was eager to die ?
Just for his country, without hope of glory,
He dropped from the saddle in darkness to lie.

Bear him in pity, and bear him in anguish ;
You think them soft lips, but they changed
without moan ;
For I, who rode next him, sprang forward and
clasped him,
And held both his hands, to the last, in my own.

We knew not the great heart that bore him right
onward,
Beating its twenty good years out so well ;
But, comrades, I felt the thin hands of his mother,
Bearing him up through my own when he fell.

Sad 't is to think of the lonely brown homestead
Set in the bleak, barren, North hills afar ;
There they have loved him so, there they will
mourn him so,
Never returning to them from the war.

THE DRUMMER-BOY OF MARBLEHEAD.

HO! arms to strike and forward feet,
  Ere dries the blood by dastards shed!
While scowls and gleaming eyes that meet
  Bewail our murdered dead.
From Berkshire's mountains to the Bay,
  Her rally Massachusetts rings,
Curse on the faltering step to day
  That shame upon her brings!

This April day which frowning dies,
  Betrothèd in its natal hour
To hills that prop New England's skies,
  Brought vengeance for its dower:
Then arms to strike and forward feet,
  Ere dries our blood by dastards shed!
For men, upon each village street
  Are mustering, as at Marblehead.

Pauses a homeward schoolboy there;
  Absorbed in thought he stands;
While patriots pass with brows of care,
  And muskets in their hands.
Then starting, to a comrade spoke
  That gallant boy of Marblehead:
"The tether of my books is broke,
  Brace me the drum instead!"

Now serried ranks are slanting grim
  Their bayonets in the summer beams ;
And, keeping step to Freedom's hymn,
  Southward the column streams.
" Your blessing, mother ! cease to cry,
  There really is no cause for dread ;
Our grand old tunes will make them fly ! "
  Said the bold boy of Marblehead.

New England's sons were smiting sore,
  With whistling ball and sabre stroke,
The rebel rout which fast before
  Fled for the swamps of Roanoke.
And in that hour of steel and flame,
  On and exultant, still there led,
While falling foemen felt his aim,
  The drummer-boy of Marblehead.

" Once more we 'll have our good old air,
  'T is fitting on this glorious field,
'T will quell the traitors in their lair,
  And teach them how to yield ! "
It swelled, to stir our hearts like flame ;
  Then back a hostile bullet sped,
And Death delivered up to Fame
  The drummer-boy of Marblehead.

THE SOLDIER'S LITTLE DAUGHTER.

BY MRS. M. A. DENISON.

THE night was stormy, dark, and cold;
  My way led through the city,
Where wretched buildings, gray and old,
  Seemed stained with tears of pity.

Few were the cheerful sounds I heard,
  No laughter wild and free;
But once the sweet voice of a bird
  Piped up and plained to me.

A little bird unblessed with wings,
  Her dark, sad eyes all tearful;
Ah, God! to see such tender things
  Out in the storm is fearful.

And thus she plained: — "Oh! stranger hear;
  I never begged before;
But mother has been dead a year,
  And father 's gone to war.

"And yesterday the work gave out
  By which I earned a penny;
Last night I had a crust of bread;
  To-night I have n't any.

And I am very hungry, sir."
  I brought her bread — to spare —
Then up into the old gray house
  Climbed by the broken stair.

A tremulous light threw shadows long
  Over the cheerless room;
O! childhood — shrined in deathless song,
  Are such your spots of bloom?

I asked her name, her tender age;
  Intensest pity won her;
A little maid of seven years,
  And all this woe upon her!

"My name is Nelly Grover, sir;
  My father loved me dearly; —
And is it true, as people say,
  That war is ended, — nearly?"

'T was strange, but as she spoke, I chanced
  To look my paper over:
And there I read — "*Shot through the heart*
  A private, William Grover."

O, awful hour! can I forget
  Her tears, her broken sobbing;

The little heart I pressed to mine
  With bitter anguish throbbing!

And as the light grew dimmer,
  And the wild cries fainter fell;
Unto my soul there came a voice, —
  I marked its cadence well:

"I sleep beneath the traitor's sod
  I died for Liberty;
I give my spirit unto God, —
  My little child to thee.

"Teach her to hold as sacred trust
  Her patriot father's doom;
Teach her to pray that from his dust,
  Freedom's fair flowers may bloom!"

Thus to my home, most tenderly,
  With loving words I brought her;
Ah! only death could tear from me
  That soldier's little daughter.

LAST WORDS.

BY HORATIO ALGER, JR.

"DEAR Charlie," breathed a soldier, —
  "O, comrade, true and tried,
Who in the heat of battle
  Pressed closely to my side;
I feel that I am stricken,
  My life is ebbing fast;
I fain would have you with me,
  Dear Charlie, till the last.

"It seems so sudden, Charlie;
  To think to-morrow's sun
Will look upon me lifeless,
  And I not twenty-one!
I little dreamed this morning
  'T would bring my last campaign;
God's ways are not as our ways,
  And I will not complain.

"There 's one at home, dear Charlie,
  Will mourn for me, when dead,
Whose heart — it is a mother's —
  Can scarce be comforted.

You'll write and tell her, Charlie,
With my dear love, that I
Fought bravely as a soldier should,
And died as he should die.

"And you will tell her, Charlie,
She must not grieve too much;
Our country claims our young lives,
For she has need of such.
And where is he would falter,
Or turn ignobly back,
When Duty's voice cries 'Forward!'
And Honor lights the track?

"And there's another, Charlie,
(His voice became more low,)
When thoughts of *her* come o'er me,
It makes it hard to go.
This locket in my bosom,
She gave me just before
I left my native village,
For the fearful scenes of war.

"Give her this message, Charlie,
Sent with my dying breath:
To her and to my banner,
I'm 'faithful unto death.'

And if, in that far country
  Which I am going to,
Our earthly ties may enter,
  I 'll there my love renew.

" Come nearer, closer, Charlie ;
  My head I fain would rest,
It must be for the last time,
  Upon your faithful breast.
Dear friend, I cannot tell you
  How in my heart I feel
The depth of your devotion, —
  Your friendship strong as steel.

" We 've watched and camped together
  In sunshine and in rain ;
We 've shared the toils and perils
  Of more than one campaign ;
And when my tired feet faltered
  Beneath the noontide heat,
Your words sustained my courage, —
  Gave new strength to my feet.

" And once, — 't was at Antietam, —
  Pressed hard by thronging foes,
I almost sank exhausted
  Beneath their cruel blows, —

When you, dear friend, undaunted,
  With headlong courage threw
Your *heart* into the contest,
  And safely brought me through.

"My words are weak, dear Charlie,
  My breath is growing scant;
Your hand upon my heart — there,
  Can you not hear me pant?
Your thoughts I know will wander
  Sometimes to where I lie:
How dark it grows! True comrade
  And faithful friend, good-by!"

A moment, and he lay there
  A statue pale and calm,
His youthful head reclining
  Upon his comrade's arm.
His limbs upon the greensward
  Were stretched in careless grace,
And by the fitful moon was seen
  A smile upon his face.

THE FURLOUGH.

ANONYMOUS.

ONCE more the music of his step
  Rings on the gravel path.
Once more I meet his living eyes,
  And hear his boyish laugh.
Once more one arm is round me thrown,
  But through my tears I see
The other palsied by his side, –
  His badge of loyalty.

Day that I did not hope to see;
  Yet over all the bliss
There hangs a web of memory
  Not all unlike to this.
I'm thinking of a dream that came
  When she had passed away, —
One star, whose vanishing so turned
  To night our summer day.

I dreamed, amid the garden walk
  I wandered when a child,
Her face looked out amid the flowers,
  And on me sweetly smiled.

I clasped again the tiny form,
  As mothers only may,
And yet, and yet, I sighing sobbed,
  With me she cannot stay.

Her mission here is past, I said;
  And fragrance from the flowers,
A fancy strange, she gathered up,
  I thought, for heavenly bowers.
Unlike the scene, yet similar,
  The fountain of the tear
That rises at the sight of him,
  My sturdy volunteer.

Too short these golden autumn days
  So canopied with blue;
The hours drop as the dropping leaves, —
  As glorious their hue.

We almost bless the fatal aim
  That felled the stalwart arm,
And gave us for a year of pain,
  These days of sunny calm.
But soon the unnerved pulse will feel
  The hero-current flow,
And then the soul will mount again
  To meet the dreadful foe.

O, not alone for fireside bliss,
  And not for pleasant toys,
Are we to train our darling girls,
  Our lion-hearted boys.
Some beckon us to heavenly seats
  Amid celestial choirs;
While through the night we pray for some
  Around the lone camp-fires.

Bridgeport, Conn. E. A. B. L.

SPRING AT THE CAPITAL.

THE poplar drops beside the way
  Its tasselled plumes of silver gray;
The chestnut points its great brown buds, impatient
    for the laggard May.

  The honeysuckles lace the wall;
  The hyacinths grow fair and tall;
And mellow sun, and pleasant wind, and odorous
    bees are over all.

  Down-looking in this snow-white bud,
  How distant seems the war's red flood!
How far remote the streaming wounds, the sicken-
    ing scent of human blood!

Nor Nature does not recognize
This strife that rends the earth and skies;
No war-dreams vex the winter sleep of clover-
heads and daisy-eyes.

She holds her even way the same,
Though navies sink or cities flame;
A snow-drop is a snow-drop still, despite the nation's
joy or shame.

When blood her grassy altar wets,
She sends the pitying violets
To heal the outrage with their bloom, and cover it
with soft regrets.

O, crocuses with rain-wet eyes,
O, tender-lipped anemones,
What do you know of agony, and death and blood-
won victories?

No shudder breaks your sunshine trance,
Though near you rolls, with slow advance,
Clouding your shining leaves with dust, the anguish-
laden ambulance.

Yonder a white encampment hums;
The clash of martial music comes;

And now your startled stems are all a-tremble with
the jar of drums.

Whether it lessen or increase,
Or whether trumpets shout or cease,
Still deep within your tranquil hearts the happy
bees are humming "Peace!"

O flowers! the soul that faints or grieves,
New comfort from your lips receives;
Sweet confidence and patient faith are hidden in
your healing leaves.

Help us to trust, still on and on,
That this dark night will soon be gone,
And that these battle-stains are but the blood-red
trouble of the dawn —

Dawn of a broader, whiter day
Than ever blessed us with its ray, —
A dawn beneath whose purer light all guilt and
wrong shall fade away.

Then shall our nation break its bands,
And, silencing the envious lands,
Stand in the searching light unshamed, with spot-
less robe, and clean, white hands.

THE REGIMENT RETURNED.

BY PARK BENJAMIN.

THE fife blows shrill, the drum beats loud;
  I hear the tramp of many feet
  Come echoing up the city street,
With cheers and welcomes from the crowd.

It is the regiment returned
  That went away three months ago;
  Fearless they met the Southern foe,
And with true patriot ardor burned.

Their looks and dress are somewhat worn;
  But every gun is free from rust,
  And that is honorable dust
Upon their caps and knapsacks borne.

Their banner still is held on high,
  Though soiled with wind and rain and smoke,
  As bravely as when first it broke
In light, like sunrise, on the sky.

In the full front of battle shown,
  It onward led the serried files
  O'er many rough and weary miles,
Through wild, beleaguered paths unknown.

Against its folds the shot were cast,
  From hidden batteries, charged with death;
  And though its bearer held his breath,
'T was carried upward to the last.

And now, still marching where it waves,
  The bold survivors of the band,
  Returning to their own dear land,
Have left behind their comrades' graves.

But, vowing to avenge their loss,
  Soon, where those comrades fought and fell,
  They 'll meet once more, and conquer well
Beneath the Union's starry cross.

'T is right to welcome home with cheers
  These patriot soldiers, fresh from fight;
  Though some no longer greet our sight,
But claim their country's grateful tears.

For them we mourn; for these we raise
  Our happy plaudits to the sky,
  And, as their ranks come marching by,
Reward their courage with our praise.

VOICE OF THE NORTHERN WOMEN.

BY PHŒBE CARY.

ROUSE, freemen, the foe has arisen,
His hosts are abroad on the plain;
And, under the stars of your banner,
Swear never to strike it again!

O, fathers, who sit with your children,
Would you leave them a land that is free?
Turn now from their tender caresses,
And put them away from your knee.

O, brothers, we played with in childhood,
On hills where the clover bloomed sweet;
See to it, that never a traitor
Shall trample them under his feet.

O, lovers, awake to your duty
From visions that fancy has nursed;
Look not in the eyes that would keep you;
Our country has need of you first.

And we, whom your lives have made blessed,
Will pray for your souls in the fight;
That you may be strong to do battle
For Freedom, for God, and the Right.

We are daughters of men who were heroes;
  We can smile as we bid you depart;
But never a coward or traitor
  Shall have room for a place in our heart.

Then quit you like men in the conflict,
  Who fight for their home and their land;
Smite deep, in the name of Jehovah,
  And conquer, or die where you stand.

THE LATEST WAR NEWS.

OH pale, pale face! Oh helpless hands!
  Sweet eyes by fruitless watching wronged,
Yet turning ever towards the lands
  Where war's red hosts are thronged.

She shudders when they tell the tale,
  Of some great battle lost and won!
Her sweet child-face grows old and pale,
  Her heart falls like a stone!

She sees no conquering flag unfurled,
  She hears no victory's brazen roar,
But a dear face, which was her world,—
  Perchance she'll kiss no more!

Ever there comes between her sight
  And the glory that they rave about,
A boyish brow, and eyes whose light
  Of splendor hath gone out.

The midnight glory of his hair,
  Where late her fingers, like a flood
Of moonlight, wandered — lingering there —
  Is stiff and dank — with blood!

She must not shriek, she must not moan,
  She must not wring her quivering hands;
But sitting dumb and white, alone,
  Be bound with viewless bands.

Because her suffering life enfolds
  Another dearer, feebler life,
In death-strong grasp her heart she holds,
  And stills its torturing strife.

Yester-eve, they say, a field was won.
  Her eyes asks tidings of the fight;
But tell her of the dead alone
  Who lay out in the night!

In mercy tell her that *his* name
  Was not upon that fatal list,

That not among the heaps of slain
  Dumb are the lips she 's kissed.

Oh, poor, pale child ! Oh, woman heart !
  Its weakness triumphed o'er by strength !
Love teaching pain discipline's art,
  And conquering at length !

SONG OF THE SOLDIERS.

BY PRIVATE MILES O'RIELLY.

AIR — *Jamie 's on the Stormy Sea.*

COMRADES known in marches many,
Comrades, tried in dangers many,
Comrades, bound by memories many,
    Brothers ever let us be.
Wounds or sickness may divide us,
Marching orders may divide us,
But, whatever fate betide us,
    Brothers of the heart are we.

Comrades, known by faith the clearest,
Tried when death was near and nearest,
Bound we are by ties the dearest,
    Brothers evermore to be.

And, if spared, and growing older,
Shoulder still in line with shoulder,
And with hearts no thrill the colder,
Brothers ever we shall be.

By communion of the banner, —
Crimson, white, and starry banner, —
By the baptism of the banner,
Children of one Church are we.
Creed nor faction can divide us,
Race nor language can divide us,
Still, whatever fate betide us,
Children of the Flag are we!

COLUMBIA'S INVOCATION.

BY CHARLES A. BARRY.

COLUMBIA, washing out with tears
And hero-blood her only shame,
Turns to her Flag of eighty years,
Immortal in its stars and flame:
O beauteous gift of God! she cries;
Gleam out on every hill and plain!
Wave o'er my people as they rise
To win me back my fame again.

Her Eagle from his loftiest peak
  The pride of all his nature shows —
Screams wildly — with a clashing beak —
  Defiance to her gathering foes.
Aloft, he swoops on tireless wings,
  Not him can cannon-crash appall!
Through fire and smoke his anger rings,
  Accordant to her clarion call.

Then rouse, ye freemen; sound a blast
  From all your trumpets, loud and long!
Let not th' avenging time go past,
  Be swift, and terrible, and strong!
Uplift the Flag; let not a star
  Be sundered from its field of blue!
With fond lips kiss each sacred bar
  That runs our deathless emblem through,

And, God be with you! Hasten on!
  With martial pæans rend the sky!
Let bayonets glisten in the sun,
  And all your battle-banners fly!
And smite to kill! See! Freedom bleeds!
  She calls you with her stifled breath!
Rebellion to her temple speeds:
  March on, to Victory or Death!

THE NORTHERN VOLUNTEERS.

BY GEORGE BOWERYEM.

WE arm by thousands strong,
To battle for the Right,
And this shall be our song,
As we march into the fight:
With our country's banner o'er us,
And traitor ranks before us,
Let Freedom be the chorus
Of the Northern Volunteers!
Now hearken to the cheers
Of the Northern Volunteers!
[Chorus of cheering.]

When the battle rages round,
And the rolling of the drum
And the trembling of the ground
Tell usurpers that WE COME!—
Then the War's deep-mouthed thunder
Shall our lightnings cleave asunder,
And our enemies shall wonder
At the Northern Volunteers!
Shall wonder at the cheers
Of the Northern Volunteers!

True, loyal sons are we
  Of men who fought and died
To leave their children free,
  Whom dastards now deride!
    Tremble, traitors! at the beaming
    Of our starry banner gleaming,
    When, like a torrent streaming,
      Come the Northern Volunteers!
    Dealing death amid their cheers,
      Come the Northern Volunteers!

When Northern men unite,
  Heart to heart and hand to hand,
For Freedom's cause to fight,
  Shall Wrong the Right withstand?
    With our country's banner o'er us,
    And rebels base before us,
    And Liberty the chorus
      Of the Northern Volunteers, —
    How terrible the cheers
      Of the Northern Volunteers!

Where Freedom's banner waves,
  Over land or over sea,
It shall not cover slaves!
  They shall touch it and be free!
    Tremble, tyrants! at the flashing

Of our arms, when onward dashing,
You shall hear their fetters crashing,
Broke by Northern Volunteers!
And your slaves give back the cheers
Of the Northern Volunteers!

God of Freedom! give Thy Might
To the spirits of Thy sons!
To their bayonets in fight!
To the death within their guns!
Make their deeds in battle gory
Burn and brightly shine in glory,
When the world shall read the story
Of the Northern Volunteers!
And echo back the cheers
Of the Northern Volunteers!

COMING HOME.

ANONYMOUS.

THEY are coming home, coming home, —
Brother and lover, father and son,
Friend and foe, — they are coming home
To rest, for their work is done.

They come from the hospital, picket, and field, —
  From iron boat and frowning fort, —
In silent companies, slowly wheeled,
  In the rhythm of a doleful thought.

This was a father of women and men,
  Gray-haired, but hale, and strong of limb;
The bayonet flashed and flashed again,
  And the old man's eyes grew dim.

Here was a form of manly grace;
  The bomb-shell groaning through the air
Drenched with his blood a pictured face
  And a curl of silken hair.

This was a bright-eyed, venturesome boy;
  Back from the perilous picket-ground
They bore him, waked from his dream of joy
  To a ghastly, fatal wound.

And thus for three days lingering,
  He talked in wandering, rapid speech,
Of mother and home, and the cooling spring
  His lips could almost reach.

They are coming home: but not as they went,
  With the flying flag and stirring band;

With the tender word and message sent
From the distant waving hand.

AFTER ALL.

BY WILLIAM WINTER.

THE apples are ripe in the orchard,
The work of the reaper is done,
And the golden woodlands redden
In the blood of the dying sun.

At the cottage-door the grandsire
Sits pale in his easy-chair,
While the gentle wind of twilight
Plays with his silver hair.

A woman is kneeling beside him;
A fair young head is pressed,
In the first wild passion of sorrow,
Against his aged breast.

And far from over the distance
The faltering echoes come
Of the flying blast of trumpet,
And the rattling roll of drum.

And the grandsire speaks in a whisper:
  "The end no man can see;
But we give him to his country,
  And we give our prayers to Thee."

The violets star the meadows,
  The rose-buds fringe the door,
And over the grassy orchard
  The pink-white blossoms pour.

But the grandsire's chair is empty,
  The cottage is dark and still;
There 's a nameless grave in the battle-field,
  And a new one under the hill.

And a pallid, tearless woman
  By the cold hearth sits alone,
And the old clock in the corner
  Ticks on with a steady drone.

THE END.